The Novels of Virginia Woolf

The Novels of Virginia Woolf

B. Sudipta

PRESTIGE

Published by
Prestige Books
3/28, East Patel Nagar, New Delhi 110 008
in association with
Indian Society for Commonwealth Studies
New Delhi

Rs. 500
Prestige Books
International

ISBN: 81-85218-14-5

Jacket design by
3-A Corporation,
New Delhi 110 002

Phototypesetting by
data culture
New Delhi 110 065
Ph. 6431070

Printed at
Mehra Offset Press
New Delhi 110 002

Contents

Preface

Virginia Woolf offers a unique vision of the world by presenting a web of interrelated ideas and a network of images and suggestions as the notion of a group-mind. While being extraordinarily receptive to the major currents of thought in her age, especially those of William James about inner life and sensations, she evolves a special theory of her own. The halo of consciousness surrounding her characters is always impinging on the individual-being which is an encroachment by the group-consciousness. Virginia Woolf's theory of the group-consciousness, however, establishes a major divergence from the principle of William James who believed in the privacy of each individual's inner life. In Virginia Woolf's works, there is a tension between the individual's inner life and the concept of a group-feeling. This type of a theory seemed to have been very much in vogue at the time when Virginia Woolf and the members of the Bloomsbury Group started their literary career. I have attempted to analyze the novels of Virginia Woolf in the background of this concept. The centre of Virginia Woolf's artistic sensibility is the need for consciousness to establish its identity and integrity, and the exposure of consciousness to a constant attack of impressions and feelings, which have the capacity to vitalize, over-excite and, at the same time, destroy and deaden consciousness.

The first chapter, "A Dome of Many-Coloured Glass," is an attempt to describe the changing pattern of modern fiction from the traditional to the modern forms. The title, a line from Shelley's *Adonais*, is indicative of Virginia Woolf's preoccupation with the globe and dome symbolism which her protagonists use to denote life and reality which constantly infringes on the individual consciousness.

The second chapter, "The Initial Awakening," is a study of Virginia Woolf's early novels when she was still in search of a technique and method while trying to express and establish the need for the survival of the individual sensibility. In the two novels *The Voyage Out* and *Night and Day*, Virginia Woolf has experienced the initial awakening for the need to explore the inner world of an individual and the outer world of social responsibilities and modes of communication which intrude and hamper personal thought and vision. These two novels also indicate Virginia Woolf's apprehension of the two temporal realities of space and time.

The third chapter, "The Edge of Consciousness," is a study of three novels: *Jacob's Room*, *Mrs. Dalloway* and *To the Lighthouse*. I have grouped these novels together as they are remarkable for their vision and style and also because they indicate that Virginia Woolf was no longer experimenting with the form of the novel but that she was establishing her concept of life and reality in her writings. Thus life is not a "series of gig-lamps," it is the state between consciousness and unconsiousness—the edge of consciousness. *Jacob's Room* marks the realization of her individual style and Virginia Woolf ventures to present themes and techniques which would be further exemplified in her two later novels. In *Jacob's Room*, she depicts an individual defining and underlining the difficulty of apprehending the inner vision of any person. In *Mrs. Dalloway*, Virginia Woolf further perfects this technique. It is in this novel that she develops the idea that individual mood and thought influence perception, thereby highlighting enduring truths which are beyond the horizon of the material world. The individual consciousness intruding upon the collective consciousness and vice versa is a literary device that Virginia Woolf perfects in this novel and in the process she is able to give her theory of the universal-consciousness which, like an envelope, covers or enfolds life and reality. This technique is further developed and perfected in *To the Lighthouse* where Virginia Woolf goes to the extent of proving that the influence of the individual personality and consciousness continues even after death. Mrs. Ramsay is an extension of Mrs. Dalloway but in her isolation she becomes a more perfect universal perceiver. Besides, the emotion that Mrs. Ramsay is able to rouse in others is identified with the power and significance of the consciousness and the ease with which it is communicated by being diffused through the external world around her. Virginia Woolf seems to suggest that people are not distinct beings and that there is an extended awareness which binds them together. The consciousness of an individual is not a distinct and water-tight compartment and there is a constant interaction and communion between the consciousness of different individuals.

The fourth chapter, "The Conflicting Self," is a study of *Orlando*, a novel which is a fantasy and therefore cannot be grouped with any other novel. Besides, this novel, though it deals with Virginia Woolf's problems of being a woman in a typically male-domiated society, can be considered an interlude in her career as a novelist.

Chapter Five, "The Semi-transparent Envelope," is a study of the novels, *The Waves, The Years* and *Between the Acts.* The title is a line from Virginia Woolf's essay on "Modern Fiction" where she describes life and reality as a "luminous halo" and "a semi-transparent envelope." It is significant to note that she develops a very lyrical and poetical style and that she concentrates on the problem of the individual and how it is destroyed by the constrictions and demands of society. These three novels outline a new type of integration in a decaying and moribund society. What is so striking and significant is the view that individual vision depends on a shared vision and an intercommunication. This integrated vision not only affects individual-consciousness but also communal life.

Chapter Six, "The Final Appraisal," is an assessment of the final achievement of Virginia Woolf as a novelist.

The Dome of Many-Coloured Glass

The end of the nineteenth century and the beginning of the twentieth century disrupted the complacent and material thought of the Victorians. Besides, the basic philosophical attitude which had been triumphantly built up on the edifice of science suffered a rude shake-up. The reign of Darwin, Huxley and Haeckel had dawned on modern culture like a second renaissance; their doctrines had promised creativity and then led to socialism, politics and the investigation of moral and religious controversy. Novelists, dramatists and poets like Kipling, Shaw, Bennett, Wells and Bridges had made full use of this opportunity. Meanwhile, this domination of science on the realm of creative thought was declining in authority from about the early years of the twentieth century. There arose a feeling that science might continue to explain phenomena but not existence. Karl Pearson, in the first edition of *The Grammar of Science*, defined science as the classification of facts, the recognition of their sequence and relative significance. But the facts themselves were becoming too elusive. The evolutionists were of the opinion that evolution did not solely depend on environment; life was an energy, an impulse which transcended circumstances and consequently our comprehension.

Since science was losing faith in its own finality and since evolution was unaccountable, it was felt that man could not fulfil himself through adaptation to environment, even in the social, economic, political or humanistic sense of the world. On the contrary, man must look into his own heart and there he would find a way to resist the vagaries of evolution—an impulse to fulfil aims and ideals. In the myriad forms of life—the "dome of many-coloured glass"—there must be something which corresponds to the deepest intimations of human beings, the striving towards self-expression, the instinctive kinship with animals and nature and vain susceptibility to seasonal and astral influences. Their hope lay not in adaptation but integration, not world-knowledge, but life-knowledge.

When philosophers and thinkers of the twentieth century were exclaiming "know thyself" without the least clue about where to look for the raw material, a Viennese neurologist, Sigmund Freud, was able to give poets, novelists and philosophers something to think about. He had begun to explain that our rational thoughts and attitudes were the products of education, social conditions and family life. Each individual is like a bubble blown up on the surface of a dark, deep stream which is the volume of life-energy with its cross-currents, rhythms, social and race memories, perhaps originating in pre-human sources, at any rate common to all humanity. The mind of man lives a life apart consciously adapted to environment.

Freud's influence was indirect and secondhand but none the less real. He discovered "the subconscious" to an age eager to know more about itself. In the past, other writers had penetrated with a wider sympathy into that mystery, but the artist's insight was nearly always limited by the narrowness of the reader which expected characters and situations to be clear-cut, compact or unified with unaccountable motives. Freud's scientific authority proved that sculptured effects were due to artistic simplification. Thus Freud prepared the way for the introspective novel, the interior monologue, impressionism, surrealism, and revealed possibilities in the problem play as also in the autobiographical and psychological novel.

The fascination of the twentieth-century writers was with the psychological value of speech prosody, techniques of the fictional form, and the intuitive illumination of the divinely-inspired moment of creation—the apotheosis of the novel. It is a disintegrated form of presentation, like the tachistoscopical method of T.S. Eliot in his *The Waste Land.* As Denis Donoghue writes, "It is enough to say here that from Schopenhauer to Valery, Eliot and Beckett, modern literature has tended to yield up the terminology of action and to commit itself more and more desperately to the terminology of the consciousness."[1]

Shiv K. Kumar opines that the disintegration of values in the first quarter of the century caused a deterioration of religion: "This vacuum had to be filled and thus the new writers adopted subjectivity and the desire to unravel the inner processes of the soul, hitherto unapprehended."[2] In a comprehensive analysis of the new technique Robert Humphrey has suggested that it is "as if a strong emphasis is placed on exploration of the pre-speech levels of consciousness for the primary purpose of revealing the psychic being of the characters."[3]

Twentieth-century fiction is impressionistic and photographic. Symbolism is the main technique of expressing the heightened mental and psychological awareness. Inherent solipsism has resulted in the individual's preoccupation with subjective methods and modification of traditional social and linguistic structures because it impedes our cognition of the natural processes of life and environment. The Durkheim Theory is a conception of the manner in which man exists in society which is another facet of ourselves—a counterpart of our inner beings. It is also an acceptable fact that an individual's position in the social hierarchy determines the thought-processes. Virginia Woolf's birth and her growing up in a literary atmosphere explains her tendency to an ivory-tower attitude. Her novels never deal with beggars or destitutes because her sensitive personality was already scarred with the horrors of war, the domination of the patriarchy and the resultant derogatory status of women. Thus we find that her books are "a direct quotation of the mind," to borrow a phrase from Edward Bowling.[4]

The nineteenth-century English novels were mostly objective, concerned with the exposition of the problem of man in society. The psychological novel followed in the wake of the realistic novel, and exponents like James Joyce, Joseph Conrad, Virginia Woolf and D.H. Lawrence emphasized the psychological and the inner lives of their protagonists. Virginia Woolf's aesthetic philosophy can be explained on the lines of the psychological technique, the stream-of-consciousness, which is of paramount importance. She compensated for her lack of formal education by reading extensively.

Edward Dujardin had initiated this technique in 1888, in his novel *Les Laurier Sont Coupe's*. He was a symbolist and a friend of Mallarme. His novel was the turning point for the literature of the interior monologue which concentrated on the inner processes of man—lyrically, silently, wading through the mass of inexpressed emotions. The very vibrations in the atmosphere are envisioned. It is in this flux of experience that the consciousness is portrayed along with time, experience and memories in moulding the flow of thought. Finally, it is through symbolism and imagery that the artist embodies the evanescent. Harvena Richter explains the process thus:

> An aura of emotional awareness drawn from the entire being, consciousness is more than a stream of associated ideas and feelings. It is part of a complex synthesis of the individual's total response to life. We may call this a sense of lived reality and the modes by which Virginia Woolf shows it are those by which man himself experiences this reality.[1]

Virginia Woolf turned to the Russians in search of a mode of expression. She was greatly impressed by the Russian novelists like Chekhov, Turgenev, Dostoevsky and Tolstoy who were not only masters in the art of fiction but also artists in the analysis of the soul. Just before the First World War, the four innovators appeared on the scene and introduced with great flair the new technique which outmoded the traditional style.

Of the novelists who follow the Existentialist philosophy, Franz Kafka in *The Trial* portrays the incongruity of time and the discrepancy between man's inner and outer time. Reality is an escape from the tyranny of time and an exuberance in the buoyant freedom of timelessness as in Rainier Maria Rilke's *The Notebooks of Malta* and Thomas Mann's *Magic Mountain* which are constructed on the temporal sequence of past, present and timelessness, with the supreme artistic consciousness as the background. They all achieve a unified aesthetic whole, along with Joyce's *Ulysses* and Virginia Woolf's *Mrs. Dalloway* and *The Waves*. Speaking of timeless suspension, Bergson writes, "Time is not an extended image of space, but the essence of pure reality or a principle of becoming which is reality itself."[6]

Various nuances of feelings, reification of routine existence and imprinting of fleeting sensations in our minds, with time and memory are instrumental in moulding the thought-processes:

> Every stream of conscious novel bears the seal of time projected lengthwise in nothing but space—spatial rendering of "a slice of life." Time is the mind, and is symbolically represented as a flowing river with memories and visions as its chief constituents.[7]

Time is an important leitmotif in the modern psychological novels. Malcolm Lowry's *Under the Volcano* is a Faustian masterpiece, portrayed in a single day, similar to *Ulysses* and *Mrs. Dalloway*. A perfect rendering of the consciousness of the protagonist is done by Henry James in *The Portrait of a Lady* and of Bloom by James Joyce in *Ulysses*.

Mechanism arrests the instincts of our being and writers like D.H. Lawrence project the naturalness of human beings which is man's power of physical and spiritual love. For them the novel represents a tentative acting-out in the imagination of a vision of the true values involved in human relationships. They were disgusted with the dominance of sterile intellect over the authentic emotions of human beings. The novels of James Joyce, Virginia Woolf, Dorothy Richardson and D.H. Lawrence are a complete shift from naturalism, making a path away from traditional structures of novelistic techniques.

Virginia Woolf had established herself as a critic in her *Mr. Bennet and Mrs. Brown* where she had openly criticized the Edwardians. She was of the opinion that the writers of the thirties had developed auto-analysis as a reaction to the suppression of the Victorians:

> The leaning-tower writer has the courage at any rate, to throw that little box of toys out of the window. He has had the courage to tell the truth, the unpleasant truth, about himself. That is the first step towards telling the truth about other people. By analysing themselves honestly with help from Dr. Freud, these writers have done a good deal to free us from nineteenth-century suppressions. The writers of the next generation may inherit from them a whole state of mind, a mind no longer crippled, evasive, divided. They may inherit the unconsciousness which as we guessed—it is only a guess—at the beginning of this paper, is necessary if writers are to get beneath the surface, and to write something that people remember when they are alone. For that great gift of unconsciousness the next generation will have to thank the creative, the honest egotism of the leaning-tower group.[8]

Imagery and projection of the self are the two basic phenomena of psychological novels. Ralph Freedman describes it as "a form which transcends the causal and temporal movements of the narrative within the framework of fiction," and "the frontier where the novel and the poem meet."[9]

The lyrical qualities of the stream-of-consciousness technique and interior monologue were mastered by Virginia Woolf, with motifs aided from association. The maximum projection of lyricism is the 'lyrical I.' The aesthetic needs of the author are portrayed in the subjective novel. D.H. Lawrence, Virginia Woolf, James Joyce and Dorothy Richardson developed a poetic perspective; Proust transformed his memories to a richly embroidered fabric. The protean self reflects the metaphysical characteristics with heightened perception of the misery and joys of life, in the protagonists of all these novelists. Since the lyrical novel requires delicate workmanship, Alan Kennedy writes that "the inner self is formulated in language to become the Self."[10] Milton and Shakespeare also project themselves in all their creations. The feeling of ambiguity encompasses us. When reality surpasses our senses, the lyrical mode of writing captures moments of time and transcends all barriers to express the author's feelings. This is a highly individualized response to life's experience.

A glimpse into Virginia Woolf's background will enable us to see her in a better perspective. Young Virginia often had the "Cream of Literatteurs" for company, her father being the famous Sir Leslie Stephen. She also had his library at her disposal. Her home atmosphere was one of agnosticism, interwoven with the fine artistic sensibility of her mother. Due to this background, Virginia Woolf was criticized as an ivory-tower aesthete with high-brow sentiments. University education was male prerogative and a woman had no right to the precincts of the university. The woman's Suffragette movement reached its zenith in the year 1911 and Virginia Woolf naturally gravitated towards it, in retaliation against the dominating patriarchy. The only solution she felt to end this oppression was to adopt the theory of "androgynous mind," which was the union of the artistic sensibility of the female and the scientific faculty of the male. Her aesthetic theory traverses deeper into the labyrinthine depths of the mind—the conscious and the unconscious. The unconscious, along with the shy and elusive imagination, lends coherence to the amorphous mass of conscious registration of the mind. Freud considered the unconscious as "psychic reality"—the basis of Virginia Woolf's creativity.

Virginia Woolf was a prominent member of the Bloomsbury Group, a group of twentieth-century brilliant scholars from Cambridge. Members of this group were aesthetically-inclined people, well-placed and involved in acts of creativity and enlightenment of their sensibility. Virginia Woolf was the nucleus of the group which consisted of famous writers like Lytton Strachey, Maynard Keynes, Leonard Woolf, E.M. Forster, Clive Bell and Desmond McCarthy. They detested materialism and prudery, preferring their informal and unrestrained atmosphere. This coterie of writers shared a common interest in love, art and truth and a common revulsion against the cramping inhibitions of the middle-class Victorian mind. The philosophy underlying the members of the Bloomsbury Group in their manner of communication is beautifully put forward by Nigel Nicolson in these thought-provoking lines from Khalil Gibran:

> Love one another, but make not a bond of love
> Fill each other's cups but drink not from one cup
> Let there be spaces in your togetherness.[11]

Nigel Nicolson has referred to Bloomsbury as a reality which has left us a legacy, the gift of friendship. She joined the group around 1910, at the time when Henry James was reigning supreme who was of the opinion that the imaginative mind could convert the very pulses of the air into revelations.

Jung's most important contribution to psychology is the theory of Eros and Anima; the female archetypes should harmonize with the male archetypes—Logos and Animus. This is the origin of androgyny. The gender norms had to be transcended or the negative effects of insanity and incarceration would be the result. Women novelists like Elizabeth Bowen, Doris Lessing, Anne Porter, Jean Rhys and Fay Weldon have also voiced similar opinions.

Anthony Burgess referred to the genders as Yin and Yang, pertaining to Chinese Philosophy.[12] A novelist is aware of his/her sex in normal existence. But once the diurnal atmosphere is transcended, the novelists do not apprehend the gender barrier and like Tiresias are transformed to hermaphrodites. Yin predominates in the books of most women writers like Rosamond Lehmann, Dorothy Richardson, Bowen, Woolf, which are powerful expressions of resentment against the male patriarchy. Woolf's social vision advocates the law of equal association. Peggy in *The Years* associates life with a Conradian vision of darkness, the negative and fruitlessness of existence. A hypostatised society bears equivalent principles like subject-object reality. Lawrence's theory is similar to Woolf's androgynous theory of the dualism of the male-female principles.

The key to the proper understanding of the novels of Virginia Woolf lies in her symbolism. She is respected for her originality and honesty in attempting to find some stability in the eternal flux and fluidity of life. She was of the opinion that symbols were to be used and then boldly discarded, or one had to face the threat of their losing the originality and evocative powers, and becoming faded metaphors. Her symbolizations are at variance from Freud's dream symbols or Jung's archetypes. Freud in his book *Interpretation of Dreams* terms symbols as "Unconscious Ideation." Virginia Woolf's views coordinate with those of Thomas Hardy also who represents fellow-beings by their own passions and idiosyncracies. George Meredith, though a Victorian, also brings forward nature to symbolize thoughts and feelings. It was in her illness that Virginia Woolf experienced the mysticism that so fills her works. Her novels are psychological studies of the protagonists with the aid of symbols:

> The centre of Virginia Woolf's artistic sensibility is the need of consciousness to establish its identity and integrity, and vulnerability of consciousness to the constant barrage of impressions and feelings which can on the one hand vitalize, but on the other, overexcite, destroy or deaden consciousness. The focus on consciousness is so great that it becomes the centre of the self: the self primarily is defined by the character of the consciousness, by the manner in which the world is perceived, by the memories and moods, which activate or inhibit the flow of consciousness.[13]

Walter Allen portrays the Woolfian art of projecting characters:

> How to impose significance on the flux? In all of Virginia Woolf's novels is this very question. When one thinks in the abstract of a typical Virginia Woolf's character, one seems to see a tiny figure on tip-top eagerly grasping a butterfly-net, alert to snare the significant, the transcending moment as it flies. Mrs. Woolf's characters are always in search of a pattern

> of meaning through them.[14]

Woolf's characters are intensely aware of the moment lending an aura of transience to the narrative. The physical world is apprehended in a sensual yet ethereal form in a recapitulative mood woven into the present. Her novels give a feeling of bubble-like evanescence, with its lyricism and revelations.

Virginia Woolf's main obsession was with life and the inner meaning of reality. She attempted to delve into its inconceivable depths; thus her protagonists have often voiced similar questions "Who I am, What I am, and so on: these questions are always floating about in me."[15] She envisioned life in a manifested form—"a luminous halo, a semi-transparent envelope"[16] She portrayed life on a similar plane as Spenser, Keats and Walter Pater, as everchanging, protean and mutable. Writing about *Jane Eyre* and *Wuthering Heights*, Virginia Woolf explains how the rising passions had to be expressed at the very moment which was possible only by symbolism:

> to feel the need of some powerful symbol of the vast and slumbering passions in human nature than words or action can convey.[17]

Modernity lies in the subtlety of sensibility and fine recordings of indistinct sensations. Religion is either ignored or finely interlaced, as in all the novels of Virginia Woolf. Man's values and principles are undergoing a steady metamorphosis, like accepting D.H. Lawrence's embodiment of life in sex, while projecting it from a philosophical angle. James Joyce's style was unique as in *Ulysses* and *Finnegan's Wake* which was like an awakening of the human soul. Virginia Woolf's concern too was to draw out the maximum essence from the flux of time and also the sensibilities of life. Mechanism arrests the instincts of our nature and D.H. Lawrence's theory of "blood consciousness" projects the naturalness of human beings which is man's power of physical and spiritual love.

The concept of death can be analyzed from various angles. From an individualistic point of view, we can gauge the concept of death viewed from a state of anxiety, frustration or an attitude of resignation, assuring a physical release from all worldly problems.[4] The pivotal role to determine one's attitude towards death is the role one plays in society. Most often one's concept of death governs our behavioristic pattern. A positive attitude is related to an optimistic personality. A negative attitude reflects a pessimistic mode of thinking and behaviour.

The root cause of the formation of particular concepts is the prior perception of death-situations by way of frequent exposure to death. The emotional responses which follow automatically mould certain impressions in the mind. Frequent bereavements in the life of Virginia Woolf affected her entire life. These emotional disturbances and bereavements are expressed in different forms and sequences. The most prominent portrayals are in the garb of insanity and death. Death is related to philosophy, at times to even a greater degree than life. Death is an unseen aspect in oblivion into darkness, a complete break from the living, giving ample scope to philosophizing into the depth of the unfathomable abysses, its ambiguities and mysteries.

Virginia Woolf suffered from schizophrenia which is psychic death with suicidal tendencies resulting from childhood bereavements and social injustice to women, of which she herself was a victim. Psychological inaccessibility is sensitized by certain social practices—partiality to men, their dominant attitudes and the resultant social pressures on women. Suicide relates to psychological and social factors which contribute considerably in analyzing this self-destructive notion. Certain social norms inflict permanent injury to particularly sensitive individuals.

Kardiner's fundamental concept is "basic personality," which is defined as "that personality configuration shared by the bulk of society's members because of the early experiences they have in common. . . . Frustrations in childhood are responsible for the modifications of personality that in adult life will constitute unconscious character patterns."[18]

As life is important, so is death. The cycle of life is never complete without death. James Joyce, Virginia Woolf, Thomas Mann and Marcel Proust have rendered death romantically. All poles of being have to be gauged realistically from daily existence which includes insanity, grotesque experiences and war. In Ernest Kreuder's delightful fantasy *Enter without Knocking*, the hero is a voluntary paying guest in a sanatorium. Most of the modern novels deal with abnormal conditions of the mind. Insanity spells extreme individualization; a condition of pathologically exaggerated sensibility which is subjectivism carried to an extreme. William Faulkner mirrors complex states of mind like that of Benjy, the idiot in *The Sound and the Fury*. This is a dangerous symbol of decline. Franz Kafka's diaries reveal his psycho-neurotic nature because of the excessive domination of his father, depicting pain and torture of the mind. Virginia Woolf's neurotic condition too has been widely discussed as it has been very conspicuously portrayed in *Mrs. Dalloway* where Septimus Warren Smith is Virginia Woolf's sensitive other self, downtrodden by the invisible shackles of society. She visualized intelligently and accurately the externalities and the hidden depths of life. Her writings were substantially on a more sensitive and higher plane of thought and thus appealed mainly to the intelligentsia.

Katherine Mansfield and Virginia Woolf shared many characteristics. Both suffered from ill-health and depression. They longed for normal healthy lives but fate ordained otherwise. Even their desire for motherhood remained unfulfilled. Virginia Woolf noted in her diary that she would remember Katherine Mansfield all her life as she found many things in common with her which she found in nobody else. Katherine Mansfield too shared these sentiments and communicated these to Virginia Woolf in a letter:

> We have got the same job Virginia, and it is very curious and thrilling that we should both, quite apart from each other, be after so very nearly the same thing.[19]

External influences and contemporary writers had a tremendous effect on Mrs. Woolf's artistic ventures. Jean Guiguet comments that Butler looms too large in Woolf's background, to be omitted. The novels that have been fertilized by *Way of All Flesh* must by this time constitute a library.[20] Virginia Woolf comments in her biography:

> Literature was suffering from a plethora of old clothes. Cezanne and Picasso had shown the way. Similarly writers should fling representation to the winds, and follow suit.

Roger Fry, who says that Truth is the fusion of vision and design, had a considerable influence on Virginia Woolf.

The twentieth-century novelists were chiefly concerned with depicting reality. The influence of the French realists and naturalists—Balzac, Zola, Flaubert and Maupassant on Joyce, Virginia Woolf, Lawrence and Conrad cannot be disregarded. Lawrence's "blood consciousness" was "the luminous halo" of Virginia Woolf. The Post-Impressionist paintings of Cezanne, Picasso, Matisse, Renoir, Degas and Manet arouse the consciousness of a new and definite reality. Virginia Woolf's contemporaries who echoed her sentiments and believed in the 'isness' of things were Joyce, Andre Gide, Thomas Mann, Franz Kafka and William Faulkner.

Kant's Theory of Reconciliation elevated the subjective sensibility to transcendental heights, enabling the transmutation of his aesthetic sensibilities to be manifested, absorbing the universe in their being and portraying it, as Virginia Woolf did in the characters of Peter Walsh, Percival, Carmichael, Miss La Trobe and North who were all wanderers in space and time. Their lifestyles are projected in a fragmentary style, depicting the flux and instability of life.

Adler's theory is that an individual's opinions of himself and the world directly affect his psychological schemata which in other words is his mental framework. Another important factor is that it is impossible to consider an individual's psyche, by assessing him as an independent person who is completely segregated from society. An isolated human being cannot be a perfectly normal individual. Life, varied interests, values, problems are all social-based aspects of life which call for social interaction. This is the yardstick for adjudging one's personality. If an individual is not at par with the social standards, he develops an inferiority complex. On the contrary, if the assessment of his personality is on a higher level, then he suffers from a superiority complex. Therefore man's existence in society is governed by his psyche, resulting in adjustment or maladjustment, according to his own personal values and vision. Society terms them accordingly, just as the extremely individualistic people are considered as neurotics and social failures.

Depth psychology was originally discovered by Sigmund Freud and he termed it Psychoanalysis. The triumvirate in this field were Freud, Adler and Jung. Later Adler and Jung branched out and developed theories of their own.

Freud's theory of objective psychology is based on tough-minded individuals whereas Adler's theory of subjective psychology deals with tender-minded people. The latter is similar to William James's Theory of Antithesis which means distinguishing between the above two theories.

Freud, Adler and even Nietzsche acceded to the instinct of "drive psychology" in every human being. The manifestation of a single drive in an individual originates from two or more drives. But the expression of these drives is determined by the state of consciousness and social conditions and the individual's motivation. It is from these "drives" that one defines a personality.

Adler's postulation of a super-ordinated dynamic force which was the aggression drive became the principle force of motivation. This is brought into focus when a primary urge in an individual remains insatiated. Refined aggressive drives are games projecting a tendency to dominate religious and social conflicts. The reversal of this drive results in humility, submission and suicide. This is the fundamental drive transforming normal conscious activities like perception, sensation and interests into aggressive paths. Pure and unfiltered aggressive drives are envisaged in historical attacks, temper tantrums and paranoia, neurosis and suicide. Virginia Woolf was a victim of these unfortunate mental diseases. She was also acquainted with Freud's books on psychology.

The Freudian transition served as a saviour from nineteenth-century moralism, into a consciousness of our selves. Sophisticated psycho-analysts like Thomas Syasz, Eric Berne, R.D. Laing constitute a kind of Gestalt of new theories and attitudes similar to Freud's transitional theories which contributed to popular consciousness. Thus, Berne writes, "For certain fortunate people there is something which transcends all classifications of behaviour and that is awareness." Such people are often misunderstood by society and are considered abnormally perceptive. The individual is considered to be a psychotic because he holds different notions about social reality. Many social theorists define the world into two categories—individualism and collectivism. In this polarity of social dynamics, individual versus society, the individual who desires to be "different" is subdued by socialistic powers like the psychiatrists. As Syasz writes, this presentation can be evaded by the theories of the new consciousness.[22]

Sociology promotes the fundamental knowledge regarding man and society. Cicourel's *Cognitive Sociology* is about an individual's behaviour according to his established role in society, a cognitive centre wherein the individual is briefed about his actions, giving rise to "surface structures" from the base of the "deep structures," which are inherent parts of the protean self.[23] A dualistic personality, on the other hand, retains its individuality and accepts social norms. While opposing the tradition-based rules, the individual forges new inroads of creativity into the sphere of life. This inner agony of the consciousness, the protean self, is heightened in modern novels. Katherine Lever writes:

> One of the troublesome facts of life is that my inside is always in contact with other people's outside. I am always inside myself but outside of others. The world of many a novel turns on this point of interaction between an inner and an outer novel.[24]

Individual-consciousness is determined by an individual's perception. But the perception of various individuals, when conglomerated to a point, constitutes the group-consciousness. These are the two forces with which Virginia Woolf has dealt with great artistry. "The New Dress" is woven around these motifs of consciousness. Mabel Waring is pleased with her new dress in the privacy of her room. But at the party, she realized that when viewed through people's eyes, the dress was ridiculous. There arose conflicting feelings in her being but pride would not allow her to accept the truth. The only solution to this dilemma was to adopt a ratiocinative attitude, between one's personal visions and society's perception.

Social menaces like the subjugation of women hinder perfect interaction within society. For Rhoda and Rachel, death was the only means of escape from these societal norms. Jane Austen's characters are not wholly involved with society and could thus adjust comfortably. But Virginia Woolf's and D.H. Lawrence's characters were embedded in society and struggled for their personal identity so as to integrate their vision of reality within society.

Virginia Woolf projected the psycho-physical aspects of the individual. The earlier attempts made to portray the inner workings of the consciousness were by Henry James and the Russian writers. They rendered the dream, hypnagogic and pathological states of the protagonists. Virginia Woolf's accurate and deep psychological explorations, vivid portrayal of complex internal processes involved an extremely difficult process. This is because experience is not static and neither are our emotions which are also in a constant state of flux. Inter-relatedness of an individual to his surroundings helps in achieving his own sense of identity amidst the strange world of unknown beings. The manner of his adjustment to the various behavioural patterns is the crux of man's existence in society.

The individual in conflict with society is an ancient theme. Society's hold over the individual hampered the development of society. Ibsen's strongest individuals defy the constraints of society. Nora in *A Doll's House,* believing that an independent being is the ultimate truth, left her home, freeing herself from subjugation. Group-consciousness is a coherent systematic thought whereas individual-consciousness represents unconscious instincts and repressions. Virginia Woolf's novels are complex inner material, rendered brilliantly through the medium of evocative prose-poetry, discovering the two worlds of consciousness through the minds of her protagonists. A beautiful presentation of Woolfian architectonics where an aura of emotional awareness drawn from the entire being is shown as the part of a complex synthesis of the individual's total response to life. This can be called a sense of *lived reality* and the modes by which Virginia Woolf shows it are those by which man himself experiences this reality. By using the principles of perception and mind-function, Virginia Woolf tries to approximate the actual ways in which man sees, feels, thinks and experiences time and change and the reader, placed within the mind of the character, becomes to some extent that mind, receiving some of the emotional stimuli and sharing in its response.

In her first two novels, *The Voyage Out* and *Night and Day*, Virginia Woolf's attention is on the need for isolation which preserves the individual-consciousness, in conflict with the need to extend consciousness beyond limits set by society—a need which can be fulfilled by love. In both these novels, the need for the development of an individual sensibility is established.

NOTES

1. Denis Donoghue, *The Ordinary Universe: Soundings in Modern Literature* (London: Faber, 1968), p. 178.
2. Shiv K. Kumar, *Bergson and the Stream of Consciousness Novel* (New York: New York University Press, 1962), p. 3.
3. Robert Humphrey, "The Stream of Consciousness Technique or Genre," *Philological Quarterly*, XXX, October 1951, p. 437.
4. Edward Bowling, "What is the Stream of Consciousness Technique?," *PMLA*, CLXV, 4, June 1950, p. 345.
5. Harvena Richter, *Virginia Woolf: The Inward Voyage* (Princeton: Princeton University Press, 1970), p. 7.

6. Henri Bergson, *Matter and Memory* (London: Allen Unwin, 1912), p. 178.
7. Shiv K. Kumar, p. 9.
8. Virginia Woolf, *Collected Essays,* ed. L. Woolf (London, Chatto and Windus, 1966), II, pp. 177-78.
9. Ralph Freedman, *The Lyrical Novel: Studies in Herman Hesse, Andre Gide and Virginia Woolf* (Princeton: Princeton University Press, 1963), p. 1.
10 Alan Kennedy, *The Protean Self: Dramatic Action in Contemporary Fiction* (London: MacMillan, 1974), pp. 1 and 8.
11. Nigel Nicolson, "Bloomsbury: The Myth and Reality," in *Virginia Woolf and Bloomsbury,* ed. Jane Marcus (Hong Kong: MacMillan, 1987), p. 19.
12. Anthony Burgess, *The Novel Now: A Student's Guide to Contemporary Fiction* (London: Faber and Faber, 1967), p. 121.
13. T.E. Apter, *Virginia Woolf: A Study of Her Novels* (London: MacMillan, 1979), p. 1.
14. Walter Allen, *The English Novel* (London: The Phoenix House, 1954), p. 347.
15. *A Writer's Diary, Being Extracts from the Diary of Virginia Woolf,* ed. Leonard Woolf (London: The Hogarth Press, 1953), p. 86.
16. Virginia Woolf, *The Common Reader* (London: The Hogarth Press, 1929), I, p. 189.
17. *Loc. cit.*
18. Robert Kastenbaum and Ruth Aisenberg, *The Psychology of Death* (London: George Duckworth, 1974), p. 267.
19. Ronald Hayman, *Literature and Living: A Consideration of Katherine Mansfield and Virginia Woolf* (London: Covent Garden Press, 1972), p. 15.
20. Allen McLaurin, *Virginia Woolf: The Echoes Enslaved* (London: Cambridge University Press, 1973), p. 93.
21. Eric Berne, *Games People Play* (New York: Grove Press, 1964), p. 184.
22. Thomas Syasz, "Ideology and Insanity" in *Psychology and the New Consciousness,* ed. Ernest Keen (California: Wordsworth Publishing Co., 1972).
23. Alan Kennedy, p. 17.
24. Katherine Lever, *The Novel and the Reader* (London: Methuen, 1961), p. 75.

The Initial Awakening

Virginia Woolf's first attempt at narration, her launching into the world of the novel, was literally her "Voyage Out" into the vast ocean of this literary genre. The novel, *The Voyage Out*, published in 1915, adopts a dualistic technique, that of the traditional narrative and of the modern psychological novel. This book is singularly different from the novels published by other novelists during that period. Its technique was to expose the workings of an extraordinarily brilliant mind, and methodically portrays the innumerable dimensions of the deceptively simple external aspects of the world. Woolf's style and technique are unique since she was battling with two opposite forces which were the superficial strata and the elusive, incomprehensible layer, imperceptible to an insensitive soul. As Michael Leaska says, "An extraordinary display of a bristling mind enunciating a carefully structured, multi-levelled, image of life."[1] It is in this novel, that we get a glimpse of Virginia Woolf's initial struggle with her creative instinct and the immense, complicated subject of her creation, the human mind and humanity in general.

Virginia Stephen and Leonard Woolf were married on the tenth of August 1912 and went to France, Spain and Italy for their honeymoon. Here Leonard Woolf was shocked to discover Virginia Woolf's frigid attitude towards sex. On their return, she feverishly completed the novel and handed it over for publication; but the tension of its public acceptance, the criticism which would automatically be meted out to her, resulted in an attack of insanity. This extreme sensitivity has been portrayed in Woolf's female protagonists.

Initially, Virginia Woolf titled her book *Melymbrosia* which she had commenced writing in March 1909. It was planned as a social comedy, on the model of E.M. Forster's fictional pattern. But as the writer with an intense and intricate sensibility went on, the novel acquired a deeper meaning along with a visionary appeal. The new dimension in technique is adorned with an aura of poetry, a talent which would hold a complete sway in *The Waves*. There is no plot as such but it is the delineation of a young girl Rachel, stepping into the intricacies of social existence. She was steered into the complications of society and was engulfed by the love of Terence Hewet, a budding author. The pulse of the narrative will be the stream of their thoughts, their utterances and personal interactions, from which a definite shape will concur with the meaning, and the novel as a whole would take shape. The minds of the characters sometimes transcend their bodies, attaining extra-corporeal consciousness. At this stage, at times, we witness a diffusion of the subject-object relationships and an omniscient author presenting the varied descriptions of nature, persons and their consciousness, which is designated by the pronoun "one."

We get a clear picture of the profound depths of the author's mind. There is a mystical diffusion of human beings, animals, nature and her bounteous beauty which are all unified into a single perspective. The mysteries of darkness are more attractive to her than an illuminated space. In a letter to Lytton Strachey in 1916 she had hoped:

> to give the feeling of a vast tumult of life, as various and disorderly as possible, which should be cut short for a moment by death, and go on again—and the whole was to have a sort of pattern, and be somehow controlled. The difficulty was to keep any sort of coherence—also to give enough details to make the characters interesting.[2]

In dealing with individual psychology, Adler deals with conflicts which the individual faces amidst society and not within oneself. Virginia Woolf's problems stemmed from social disparity betwixt the two sexes which accrued in personal conflicts. This psychological setback was constantly reflected in her literary creations. The problems arising due to maladjustment in society, like neurosis, unrest and melancholia, became recurring motifs in her narrations. Her idea was to orchestrate a pattern in society which would ease the problem of the subjugation of women. Her theory of androgyny is laudable since it places man and woman at a single point of elevation.

An inferiority complex causes more damage than can be evinced superficially. It directly decreases the individual's social interests leading to psychological abnormalities. Positive psychological evolution can be processed through the recycling of many customs and traditions in accordance with changing times. This will enable improved individuality and group-interaction, for the betterment of society and mankind.

The Voyage Out is a novel which narrates the experience of a twenty-four year old girl, Rachel Vinrace when she embarked on a voyage aboard her father's ship the Euphrosyne, accompanied by her aunt, uncle, a servant and an old acquaintance, Mr. Pepper. Rachel is a young innocent girl, uninitiated into the complexities of life, a fragile picture of an undefiled maiden. Being a motherless child, her aunt Helen takes it upon herself to introduce her niece to the social graces, its experience and wisdom. The ship makes a halt at the Tagus River. We are introduced to two new characters, Mr. and Mrs. Dalloway, who board the ship. Richard Dalloway is a politician but the stormy sea momentarily disrupts his senses and he kisses Rachel in a moment of passion, his heart aflame with desire for this innocent rosebud. Rachel is terrified and dismayed, being wholly unaware of physical contact and the resultant feelings. Her initial sexual experience results in frightening delusion and consternation. Along with Helen and Ridley Ambrose, Rachel disembarks at Santa Marina where Helen had decided to educate Rachel and acquaint her with the social world and its intricacies and complexities. In the island, among the holiday-makers are two young men who become particularly friendly with them—Terence

Hewet, an aspiring author and St. John Hirst, an academician. Rachel and Hewet fall in love in due course and she experiences certain hitherto unknown feelings and nuances of the heart. The tourists venture inland in an expedition into the dense forests and rivers. Tragically, Rachel is infected by a fatal disease, becomes very sick, and finally loses consciousness and dies. The death of this innocent child on the threshold of life is profoundly tragic. The story is a conventional theme of a shipping magnate's daughter and a young novelist's love. This social portraiture reminds us of Joseph Conrad's *Heart of Darkness*. In this romantic setting Rachel meets the destined fate of all romantic young girls.

Rachel's consciousness experiences a spatial movement from the state of innocence to initial socializing and the discovery of love finally ending in death. Virginia Woolf sketches a dualistic journey—a physical voyage in space out of England to a coastal village in South America to a personal voyage in inner space.

Virginia Woolf very adroitly builds up the narrative, tracing Rachel's adaptation to life through literary means like books, symbols, music and her personal relationships with an infinite variety of characters. Terence Hewet in the novel remarks that writers usually put a good deal of themselves into their first books and this is precisely true of Virginia Woolf in *The Voyage Out* where an in-depth study brings out the autobiographical element.

The title depicts Virginia Woolf's initial voyage into the ocean of fiction, a destination for the unknown terrains of the psyche. We may view it as a personal excursion by Virginia Woolf into the psychic world of imprisoned impressions and thoughts unexpressed by the lack of an appropriate language and technique in order to release them from their fetters. Once the chains were dissolved, Virginia Woolf's thoughts cascaded down in a torrential flow of visionary images, giving us a glimpse of the romantic poet existing within her being. Her attempt had been to express reality as experienced by her.

The title itself gives us the outline of the novel and is adapted to a social atmosphere. Rachel Vinrace, disgusted with the traditional life of subservience and loneliness destined for a woman, is an ascetic at heart.

The novel commences on the embankment of the Thames, a symbolic beginning, since Virginia Woolf's stream-of-consciousness depicts life as a flowing river, a symbol of travel and voyage. The Thames is a water-passage in London with historical and literary memories. Spenser had often made references to the Thames. Gazing into its depths is like gazing into life itself. The image of the river is central to the novel, depicting the flowing consciousness and identifying Rachel's initial voyage from her limited existence into the vast world. Her nature too is reflected in the gently flowing river. Passivity was the crux of her nature. Her impressions of the outer world were simply passive reflections. She "seemed to see and hear a little of everything, much as a river feels the twigs that fall into it and sees the sky above."[3]

While embarking on this voyage, the characters are relinquishing their past and will be free of any encumbrances which determine their actions and thought-processes. Therefore, Rachel's voyage commences in a relaxed frame of mind, similar to all the other characters. Virginia Woolf adroitly manoeuvres her protagonist into an unrestricted atmosphere, providing her with a complete freedom of thought and action.

In "Modern Fiction" and *Mr. Bennett and Mrs. Brown*, Virginia Woolf calls this narrative style an experiment. It is not mere narration but the projection of an experience and a sensitive attitude wherein life is a series of sensations and experiences. The most important factor is the particular moment of enlightenment and inspiration, a point where the whole of reality becomes an open screen. The clever utilization of temporal and spatial images lends depth and intensity to the narrative.

The novel commences with the Ambroses leaving London, a place where "beauty goes unregarded, eccentricity must pay the penalty." (5) The greatest tragedy of the twentieth century is progression in the scientific and materialistic world where the response to natural beauty is lost. For the author, urbanization resulted in a degeneration of aesthetic perception, making life worthless. Therefore, she utilizes the natural elements of the universe and attempts an escape from conventional life into a psychic exploration. The novel begins with the third-person narrative, with the author presenting her viewpoint. The technique in narration is that of suspense which can profitably be compared to that of Meredith and E.M. Forster. Helen is visibly upset but the cause of this emotional upheaval is not disclosed. She was looking at a circular iridescent patch in the river with fascination and weaving her thoughts around it. Light, tone and colour cadence through her mind, forming intricate web-like thoughts—a poetic, transcendent sensation, imbuing her readers in the lilting melody of poetry. Her imagery and alliteration resemble Keats's usage of words based upon sensual imagery.

Rachel's character is paradoxical—she can neither find peace and tranquillity in solitude nor in crowds of people or a busy social life. As a lonely individual she had to cater to the whims and fancies of her two old-fashioned aunts. She had lost her mother at a very tender age and had an extremely busy father who could not spare any time for his daughter. Virginia Woolf brings this innocent girl into contact with society in a clever and planned manner through the medium of books and people.

It is only in a human institution that an individual can cultivate himself. Virginia Woolf very cleverly presents an array of characters for Rachel to transcend her inhibitions and get into the groove of society. Her uncle and aunt, Helen and Ridley Ambrose, are a well-adjusted couple even though they are poles apart by nature. Ridley is a comprehensive picture of male egotism. All the male characters seem to be reflections of Woolf's father Leslie Stephen in one form or another, Ridley was projected as a recluse scholar. Helen was an aspect of Woolf's mother Julia Stephen and initially was in an emotional turmoil on being parted from her children. But on meeting Rachel, her maternal instincts are transferred to her and she gets obsessed with the idea of grooming this innocent motherless girl. She is introduced to us on a psycho-analytical plane giving us a hint of her vulnerable nature camouflaged by her aggressive possessive nature: "It was only by scorning all she met that she kept herself from tears." (9) The crux of Helen's problem was her innate feeling of loneliness which would now be channelled into a satisfying perspective, that of conditioning Rachel's insufficiency and moulding her into a reasonable and normal individual.

Richard and Clarissa Dalloway board the ship at the mouth of the Tagus river. In their relationship, Rachel once again witnesses the dominant male and the subservient female. Clarissa could have been a portrayal of Helen Schlegel of E.M. Forster's *Howard' s End.* Clarissa would make it a point to discuss literature, be it Shakespeare, Pascal or Jane Austen, but Rachel is disgusted with Cowper's *Letters* and prefers to play the piano. But, as she confided to Clarissa, her protective aunt "would as soon have forced her to go through one piece of drudgery thoroughly as they would have told her that her hands were dirty" (29) or she would ruin her hands playing the piano. But it was music which gave Rachel emotional sustenance and a reprieve from suffocation even in solitude. When Clarissa enters the room, Rachel feels her Bach fugue crumble to the floor. This perpetual conflict within her being had to be transcended but it would be a difficult proposition. Fortunately, Clarissa's gay sprightly nature appealed to Rachel and she pleasantly realized that she could converse without inhibitions.

Every individual feels a desire to express his individuality and be himself for a few moments. Richard Dalloway was on a holiday. He escapes his political involvements and relaxes contentedly on Willoughby's ship. He was pleased with the thought of his reducing the working hours of women. This gave him more pleasure than what he would have experienced if he had composed the poems of both Shelley and Keats. His theory of unifying the social and political world implies his desire of living in harmony. But for Rachel it was not that simple and she felt alienated. Her dilemma was more profound, similar to that of Septimus Warren Smith in *Mrs. Dalloway.* Both were attempting to unite two realities, one being our individual selves and the other being social reality. Richard's theories intrigue Rachel and thus, lost in contemplation, she loses her sense of being. She forgets that she has to put in an effort to regain her impressions of reality and meanwhile is oblivious of the fact of her existence. Thus she is disenchanted with the world, losing herself in its profound immensities, and annihilating her being into nothingness: "The things that existed were so immense and so desolate." (125) She could not grapple with certain aspects of social norms which arose in the wake of her socialization. Sex is one field where senses would not consolidate and provide sensuous joy. Richard's desire for sex had been awakened due to his close proximity with Rachel which resulted in a most ardent and passionate kiss. Sexual awakening is a natural phenomenon of society where two genres cohabit. But Rachel's inexperience resulted in repression and inarticulation which destroyed all beauty and sensations of a beautiful relationship. Language is sometimes a great obstruction; the lack of appropriate words results in thoughts that cannot transcend the barriers of the mind. Initially, Rachel was physically and mentally in a turmoil but the sight of the sea filled her with serenity: "Nevertheless something wonderful had happened to her." (73) But her subconscious reaction could not be subdued and at night she had a terrifying dream. She was walking in a tunnel made of brick walls which was closing in on her and it was spotted with deformed men having long nails with faces resembling animals. Then she also imagined barbarian men pursuing her and due to these traumatic dreams, she could not sleep.

Virginia Woolf very deftly opened two avenues for the progress of Rachel's development in her inner and outer life. Fortunately, she enjoyed the company of the Dalloways and looked forward to further meetings. The lingering joy that pervaded her being could be due to her sexual awakening. Her terror and joy were a projection of her complex psyche. Rachel had received love in a diffused manner only and not the spontaneous love of a mother and the uninhibited affection of a lover. She received negative impressions on this tender mind, till fate intervened and she came aboard the Euphrosyne. In reality too, Virginia Woolf had undergone a complete emotional transformation when the family shifted residence from Hyde Park Gate to Gordon Square. Here she came into contact with many literary young men, who would all consolidate their company in the name of the Bloomsbury Group.

Water is the central symbol in almost all the novels of Virginia

Woolf. Water, sea and waves delineate her moods, experiences and meaning of life as in *The Waves*, *To the Lighthouse* and *The Voyage Out*. Water is the element which heals all wounds and washes away all impurities. Virginia Woolf was constantly tortured by the unfair treatment meted out to women. The masculine element in her thoughts is projected as destructive, creating chaos and disharmony. Women are the peaceful sex, men are egoists subjugating women to their will. Ironically, it is only a woman who can tinge the male aridity with her green-world simplicity and nurture the death-like barrenness of life. Thus Virginia Woolf fought for self-expression for women as a community and for their endangered consciousness which was threatened by the arrogant and dominant male. Water, the life-giving fluid which unifies all and merges all conflicts, was the symbol which animated her profoundly. This is the divine element which merges and unifies all polarities, like life and death, consciousness and unconsciousness. Its infinite depths are not apparent because of its purity, calm and serenity. It is symbolic of many meanings pertaining to the mysteries of life and the obscurity of the future, its own abounding mysteries and heterogeneity:

> Mr. Pepper went on to describe the white, hairless, blind monsters lying curled on the ridges of sand at the bottom of the sea, which would explode if you brought them to the surface, their sides bursting asunder and scattering entrails to the winds. (18)

The sea with its perpetual flux, its multiplicity and pluri-significance is delved into by Virginia Woolf through the portrayal of the infinite beauty and depth of her own being in the garb of her female protagonists. It is in the musings and reflections of Rachel that absurdities become meaningful, inanities assume importance, even though superficially she is portrayed as a limited and infantile person. She is constantly searching for meaning in her interaction with society. Richard Dalloway's diffused conversation intrigues her because she does not perceive the reality in it; talks of philosophy and knowledge fill her with a sense of loss. But she does respond to Richard Dalloway's company: "She stirred her tea round and round; the bubbles which swam and clustered in the cup seemed to her like the union of their minds." (53) For the first time her emotional affinity is projected and the reader comprehends that her response to society is apparently positive.

The destination is finally reached and they disembark at Santa Marina. The "loneliness of human life" terminates and they reach their beautiful white villa which is their holiday abode. Time passes and Rachel's personality too is steadily transformed. With bright eyes and a tanned complexion, she is quite confident in her manner. Her room is like a world to her. It is in religion and art that one probes for meaning; Rachel had access to religion at Santa Marina but its unreality embittered her. The only institution that could afford her even a temporary semblance of meaning is art, a resolution for the dialectic that is to be suggested again in *To the Lighthouse* and denied in *The Waves*. Rachel is a pianist whose personality in terms of mythic thought is united concretely with music which brings meaning, order and a certain unity into her existence but does so chiefly because it promotes subject-object diffusion. Rachel's diffuse experience of music includes the synesthesia of visualized music, a phenomenon which she shares with Rhoda in *The Waves*, Miss Marchmont in *Jacob's Room* and Septimus Smith in *Mrs. Dalloway.*

Literature was the most effective source of Rachel's enlightenment. She came into contact with various characters and this group-consciousness had a positive effect on her. Her individual personality was intruded upon and she was less shy and less serious. She read generously but not Defoe or Maupassant as Mrs. Ambrose suggested, but modern books. She steadily progressed from Cowper to Meredith, Ibsen and finally to modern feminist novels. She identifies herself with Diana in Meredith's *Diana of the Crossways* and she got immersed in Nora of Ibsen's *Doll's House:*

> "What I want to know," she said aloud, "is this: What is the truth? What's the truth of it all?" (122)

The slow but sure progression of her mind becomes apparent. Up to this point she had existed in a world of illusion and now she was coming into contact with reality. Jane Austen's *Persuasion* was symbolic of Rachel stepping outside her cocoon-like existence. The overtones and reminiscences with the scenes of domesticity, social gatherings and marriage being the ultimate motive are reminiscent of Jane Austen's novels.

Virginia Woolf's technique is innovative since her thought-processes have to be captured in its originality and thus its presentation necessitates the utilization of temporal, spatial, mythical and mythopoetic devices. She had referred to evocative prose because her narration draws her backward in time. These interludes fortify great emotional moments. The momentous event was the commencement of her voyage as well as the voyage itself. The author and the heroine of the novel were ordained by fate to die under tragic circumstances.

Virginia Woolf shares with Bergson and Proust the conception that time cannot stop. All of them believe that during certain experiences, time can be transcended largely through memory, enabling us to live in pure time.

Rachel Vinrace's life is reflected in a temporal experiential manner wherein she as an individual transcends all barriers of life avoiding the destructive forces in the garb of well-wishers. In *The Voyage Out,* Virginia Woolf has portrayed the whole universe in a moment, like the extinction of Hewet's candle at sunrise, the intervening hours of desolation at sunset and the artificially illuminated world at sunrise. The sound of the breakfast gong reminds us of the passage of time, arousing all from their silence and lethargic postures. The ludicrousness of human time is projected in relation to eternal timelessness and infinity. Rachel's search for meaning is laced with temporal and spatial accents, vital for any cognitive progress of the self:

> And life, what was that? It was only a light passing over the surface and vanishing, as in time she would vanish, though the furniture in the room would remain. Her dissolution

> became so complete that she could not raise her finger any more, and sat perfectly still, listening and looking always at the same spot. It became stranger and stranger. She was overcome with awe that things should exist at all. . . . She forgot that she had any fingers to raise. . . . The things that existed were so immense and so desolate. . . . She continued to be conscious of these vast masses of substance for a long stretch of time, the clock still ticking in the midst of the universal silence. (124)

This is a subjective description, with her mind hovering over externalities and then weaving the inner processes wherein the fact of her own existence is realized by her. She delineates the spatial movement and temporal dimensions by the passage of light over the world. All her cognitive processes of philosophy end with clock-time and simple reality. Her individuality is developing, since her mode of perception, which is increasing with time, comprehends the immensity of this world, the universal silence. This is how the novel transcends temporal and spatial barriers. As Jean-Paul Sartre says, "the effect is that of haemorrhaging of the space of one character into the space of another."[4]

This is the technique of projecting the world through the consciousness of the minor characters. Jean Guiguet considers the sea-voyage to be a symbolic escape from time and space "within which events are inscribed and within which we inscribe our own lives . . . consciousness reduced of what is purely inward."[5]

A direct escape from time was the expedition on the Amazon river to the primitive village, unseen by many after the Elizabethan voyagers. They were separated only a little spatially, compared to the regression of ages in time. Rachel commenced her inward journey in search for meaning in human institutions with Richard Dalloway. In Santa Marina, she did not find the social group very meaningful:

> To feel anything strongly was to create an abyss between oneself and others. . . . Let these odd men and women . . . be

> symbols. . . . It appeared that nobody ever said a thing they meant, or ever talked of a feeling they felt, but that was what music was for. (32)

It was for the first time that she was "seeing life" while strolling down Santa Marina with Helen. She witnessed an intimate scene for the first time, in the company of Hewet when Susan and Arthur were in an intimate embrace. The onlookers were both agitated and sympathetic with the lovers. Love to Rachel was pathetic making her want to burst into tears. Despite the confusion of feelings and ideas Rachel finds herself attracted to Terence, maybe because she found an escape from her loneliness and envisioned some meaning from her heterosexual relationship. Helen's intellectual and emotional influence is considerable in building up Rachel's social consciousness. But Helen projects the cynical and pessimistic side of her nature by making Rachel feel insecure. Her encounter with society never gave her the joy and serenity she had anticipated. Somewhere within her was a note of dissatisfaction unseen by any living soul:

> While all her tormentors thought that she was dead, she was not dead, but curled up at the bottom of the sea. There she lay, sometimes seeing darkness, sometimes light, while every now and then someone turned her over at the bottom of the sea. (348)

She could never involve herself wholly with people and thus maintained an attitude which kept her aloof. Thus she questioned Evelyn Murgatroyd "whether the past had hung sealed packets from branches which had to be broken, to create friendship." (122)

William James in his book *Psychology: The Briefer Course* has classified a single individual into three selves—the material one, the social one and the spiritual one. The social one interacts with society and if negatively, then it suffers the most: "a man has as many social selves as there are individuals who recognize him and carry an image of him in their minds. . . . The spiritual one (is) the entire collection of the states of consciousness."[6]

Regression and identity-crisis are the result of a deficiency of inner resources by which to create a firm position in society. Asocial tendencies sprout from a negative identity, considering society's point of view, when the individual's views do not conform to those of society. Non-conformists are automatically or rather eventually alienated. The individual's personal thought-processes are heightened but they achieve only partial satisfaction because man is fundamentally a social animal.

The ambivalent characteristics we face in the novel are Rachel's subconscious desire for solitude and her physical desire for a home and social existence. Her delirious dreams were woven around the idea of escape through water which symbolizes purity. Terence reads to her from *Comus* wherein Sabrina the Virgin is called to break the spell which the debauch Comus has cast on the Lady of Milton. Rachel was like Sabrina and stepping into the fray of normal existence would be relentless and excruciatingly painful for her. Even in her illness, the nurse became a sinister woman holding the cards of destiny.

Death had to be enforced in the novel for two reasons. One is that Rachel's individuality would be cramped if she got involved in social life. Secondly, this was a revolt against the atrocities of a patriarchal society. Death is the answer for Virginia Woolf to gain eternal solitude and freedom. Moreover, she had experienced a number of tragic circumstances wherein death had isolated her from her loved ones. Presumably, her innumerable allusions to death constitute a cathartic process to remove this evil from her mind. Eternal freedom was welcome as compared to masculine dominance. Virginia Woolf did not visualize a tame end to her novel. Thus, she retained the pure and serene mysticism of Rachel's mind. Winifred Holtby is of the opinion that Virginia Woolf "sets life against death as though to discern more clearly what it means . . . a conception of the universe and of existence."[7] Rachel's unconscious fears of sexuality and eroticism create complex crosscurrents. Her aunt's indifference after announcing her engagement shows that the life ahead is an aura of recrudescent uncertainty. She thus retreats from this sequestered world to eternal peace and serenity, gaining a permanent isolation. In illness time is limitless, flowing past incessantly; but for her, temporal and spatial factors are static, uniting her to time forever in eternity with death. Her complete reuni n with nature is expressed symbolically since she is portrayed as a maiden similar to the "green-world" archetypes. Rachel is a mystic and our social arrangements incarcerate and castigate such individuals with different consciousness. Many psychologists have worked on this problem. As a social theorist, Thomas Syasz defines the world into two categories: individualism and collectivism. There is also an inbuilt conflict between the individual and the society. When the problem of adjustment surfaces, the individual will has to interact with the socialistic forces and either be subdued or condemned. These violations are controlled by psychiatrists wherein society very serenely employs their incarcerating methods under the garb of healing.

Rachel's illness pervades the atmosphere with gloom. Even Hirst is visibly perturbed and does the needful. But, being a symbol of the rational and intellectual male, he tides over his sorrow in a short span of time. For Rachel herself, death ends all doubts, inhibitions and fears. Their physical isolation is complete, and apparently brings a tragic end for the young lovers.. But their spiritual union was complete:

> She had ceased to breathe. So much the better—this was death. It was nothing; it was to cease to breathe. It was happiness, it was perfect happiness. They had now what they had always wanted to have, the union which had been impossible while they lived.... "No two people have ever been so happy as we have been. No one has ever loved as we have loved." (360-61)

Ironically, the last two lines of the above passage are similar to Virginia Woolf's last letter to Leonard Woolf, just before her suicide in 1941. Her works are consistently based on biographical lines and life is depicted as a meaningless voyage in her books. The meaninglessness is very well depicted by Jean O. Love:

> After Rachel's death, the novel shifts back to the problem of meaninglessness. Despite Terence's illusion that they are unified and that death has brought perfect, permanent happiness and peace, the problem of meaninglessness is not resolved. The book ends as other characters debate whether Rachel's death does or does not prove that life is essentially absurd and without reason. Her death itself is a pluri-significant event, but to a prominent degree it is a way of insisting that there is no real solution for the meaninglessness of existence, or at least no solution in life. *The Voyage Out* does not say whether there is an answer in death, leaving that for future dialectic and myth.[9]

Rachel's death was tragic because she was on the verge of experiencing life in its ultimate beauty, as matrimony is the union of body and soul of two individuals. But Virginia Woolf struck a tragic note and nipped her joy in the bud. Rachel's characterization was an extension of herself where she ultimately transcended all barriers and unified herself with eternity. Relief is provided by Mrs. Paley's comic reaction to the news of Rachel's death, "'Dead?' she said vaguely. 'Miss Vinrace dead? Dear me . . . that's very sad. But I don't at the moment remember which she was. We seem to have made so many new acquaintances here'." (369)

This is Virginia Woolf's final thrust at the insignificant position of an individual in society. Life is a passing phase and one is hardly remembered. Our social identity does not necessarily fill all our inner needs. Virginia Woolf dialectically draws out Rachel's character, synchronizing her initial flight into the complicated world with the wide expanse of the blue sky, the deep sea, a variegated group of people and, aesthetically, with literature and music. Thus her mind was gently recast and her despicably enshrouded past is adroitly wiped out. This rose-bud was nurtured with love and care but she faded away as she possessed too sensitive a nature to abide in this world.

As Helen M. Lynd says: "Openness to relatedness with other persons and the search for self identity are not two problems but one dialectical process; as one finds more relatedness to other persons one discovers more of oneself; as the self of one's own identity becomes clearer and more firmly rooted one can more completely go out to others." It is not a loss of oneself, an "impoverishment" but a way of finding more of oneself when one means most to others whom one has chosen. Nor must complete finding of oneself, as Fromm and others sometimes seemed to imply, precede finding oneself in and through other persons. Identity is never wholly realized; love is never perfect. Strength to apprehend love that is beyond anxiety, beyond the need to use other persons for one's own security, beyond desire for power over others is never complete and may grow throughout life. Like identity and mutuality with others, it is a lifetime process of discovery: "In the struggle for existence in a world ruled by anxiety . . . the surrender to the . . . experience of love appears softening and therefore weakening. . . . Love experiences space as bountiful, infinite."[10] Rachel finally triumphs for she is in perfect unison with life and love, even in death.

II

Virginia Woolf's next novel *Night and Day* is an extension of *The Voyage Out* but is envisioned in a deeper strata of consciousness minus the social fetters which had bound Rachel Vinrace, the protagonist of her earlier novel. Virginia Woolf's second novel has placed the protagonist in a position that is diagonally opposite to that of Rachel. Katharine Hilbery graduates from the innocent Rachel to a girl who could adjust to society promoted by the literary atmosphere at home. This novel is virtually a continuation of Rachel's life if she had lived, married Hewet and led a social life in London while preserving her individuality not in death but on a visionary level.

The title itself is dualistic in nature denoting Virginia Woolf's dual search for reality and truth in life. Reality is an elusive pixie appearing in "moments, fragments, a second of vision, and then the flying waters, the winds dissipating and dissolving."[11]

In this novel Virginia Woolf, like one of her protagonists Mrs. Hilbery, is obsessed with Shakespeare. The title carries an aura of the great master denoting the darkened world of love and mystery as night and the illuminated part of reality as day. Shakespeare's festive comedies have been emulated, making it a social satire, but with interwoven tradition projecting the contradiction of its title. The main characters too project this contradiction, being simultaneously empirical and mythopoetical. At heart they are romanticists but due to familial and social demands, they are obliged to reorient their lives, at least superficially. Therefore we come across numerous antithetical issues, to be dealt with by the author.

Anne Thackeray Ritchie considerably influenced Virginia Woolf and her literary avocation. Virginia Woolf identified many of her personality-traits, especially her free spirit in that of her aunt. The character of Mrs. Hilbery is an acknowledged portrait of Mrs. Ritchie who is the key-figure in *Night and Day*. Carol Mackay argues that Mrs. Hilbery cuts through petty incompatibilities and misunderstandings to reveal the important realities that lie beneath them: it is she who unites the opposites of night and day.[12]

Katharine Hilbery's personality is a combination of two opposite traits. She was a philosopher living in an imaginary world and in private she indulged in solving mathematical problems—a rational intellectual occupation clubbed with an imaginative personality. Ralph Denham too possessed a dualistic personality. He had to work as a solicitor due to family pressures but his aesthetic sensibility was being tortured due to his preoccupation with material life. Just like Hewet he too had a desire to write a book. These two worlds of consciousness also are symbolical of the title *Night and Day*. The opening lines give us a glimpse of the author's line of thought:

> It was a Sunday evening in October, and in common with many other young ladies of her class, Katharine Hilbery was pouring out tea. Perhaps a fifth part of her mind was thus occupied, and the remaining parts leapt over the little barrier

of day which interposed between Monday morning and this rather subdued moment, and played with the things one does voluntarily and normally in the daylight. (7)

The two worlds of consciousness thus signify night and day. Daytime stands for the superficial and the apparent; night is the symbol of the author's private working of the mind where darkness depicts a period of intense thoughts providing an aura of mysticism. The night-world is one of love and imagination and the day-world depicts contemporary reality.

Such a dilemma can be seen in Jane Austen's *Pride and Prejudice,* George Eliot's *Middlemarch* and Emily Bronte's *Wuthering Heights.* But Woolf's novels are different in the sense that she deals with the consciousness of her protagonists and therefore the dialectical processes have to be schematized with a sensitiveness in conjunction with their personalities.

In *Night and Day,* we cannot evince any past because the temporal dimension is concentrated only on the present. The time schemata is hermeneutic because, as the events are unfolded, the meaning and the significance of the novel are revealed. The characters transcend all barriers of consciousness and situational problems and retain their individuality even while existing in society. Like Mrs. Ramsay of *To the Lighthouse,* Katharine used to slide into her fantasies even amidst company. She would immerse herself in the past among the superbly dressed men and women. Serenity would pervade all around while she heard the solemn beating of the sea upon the shore. When her thoughts used to reverse back, she would desperately attempt to join the present to the past.

Night and Day is an intellectual romance. Katharine was engaged to William Rodney, a conventional male, but ultimately falls in love with Ralph Denham who respected her individuality. The story is traditional and at the same time modernly rendered with feminism as its background. Katharine is a normal, domesticated girl, more experienced and aloof than Rachel Vinrace. Polarities are the basis of Virginia Woolf's narration, otherwise there would be no conflicts and the myriad contradictory situations of fact and illusion, freedom and bondage would be missing. Our mind is divided by the conscious and the subconscious, thus making contrarieties an inherent part of our personality. The external characteristics of the protagonists are projected in society adjusting themselves accordingly. Their inner lives extend their real selves and they thrive in silence and solitude.

Virginia Woolf presents these setbacks in a traditional set-up of a couple of conventional families whose morality was not based on any profound principles. We are gradually introduced to the characters who are similar to the people we meet every day. Slowly but intricately, we traverse the tortuous path of existence, having to deal with dual worlds of consciousness.

Katharine is an introvert, thriving in her world of fanciful imagination. Her love for Mathematics too plays a dominant role in her mental framework. She is obliged to assist her mother in her literary pursuit of writing a biography, much against her will. The biography was her grandfather's, the renowned poet Richard Alardyce. For social survival and personal freedom, Katharine gets engaged to William Rodney in spite of her awareness of his different perspective of life. Simultaneously, the author builds up her relationship with Ralph Denham, employed in Lincoln Fields who was in reality a visionary at heart. Cementing these two vulnerable souls was Mary Datchet, an independent girl employed in the Suffragette Office. Ralph proposes marriage to Mary but she refuses being aware of his feelings for Katharine. There is a fortuitous turn at this juncture—Rodney falls in love with Cassandra Otway, Katharine's cousin, and this literally makes her aware of her love for Ralph. But nothing of this controversy is mentioned to anyone while Katharine assiduously helps Rodney and Cassandra in their courtship. Prudery was prevalent, as we notice in the character of Mrs. Milvain, Katharine's aunt. She was vociferously agitated by her nephew Cyril who had fathered illegitimate children and now she was shocked at the happenings in the Hilbery home. There is of course a psychological background for such extreme concern since the writer had been denied the joys of motherhood. Virginia Woolf portrays this lack of sensitivity by virtually incapacitating one of her senses. Finally, the lovers are united and Mary gets involved in a different society for the upliftment of women. Her sentiments on feminism echo those of Jane Eyre:

> Millions are condemned to a stiller doom than mine; millions are in silent revolt against their lot. Women feel just as men feel.[13]

Feminism is directly dealt with in the characters of Mary and Mrs. Seal. However, Virginia Woolf did not encourage feminist societies and their vociferous demands for equality and emancipation. She believed that mentally, men differed radically from women. Their subservient lives angered her, as she wrote in *A Room of One's Own*, "under the shadow of the rock, these million years and now timidly crawling into the light."[14]

This intense desire for a whole civilization minus this derogatory status of women, and her theory of androgynous living were projected initially in this novel with her essay "Mark on the Wall," where she describes this novel as a melancholy search for tangibility in the abysses of the mind.[15] It deals with two trends of life—that of an individual existing in her being and also surviving in society. The first two novels are a search for individual identity and happiness within the restriction of society, but Rachel the protagonist of *The Voyage Out* could not develop an impersonal attitude and overstepped these societal barriers. Katharine of *Night and Day*, being nurtured in an atmosphere contributing to a perfect personality, survived all obstacles and could settle down in life. Fortunately, she loved a man who was a visionary and thus could respect her private world of consciousness. The subjective tone is very obvious, being of utmost importance in guiding us through the various entanglements and the variegated characters with even more complicated personalities. Virginia Woolf portrays their various characteristics with her incomparable perception. Her language is simple and attempts a straight and direct portrayal. A direct narrative technique can be presented by the authorial voice which can be seen in *The Years* and *Between the Acts*. Virginia

Woolf never does concede to violent speech or an open exhibition of extreme emotions. Subtle wording denotes the intensity of feelings.

Virginia Woolf can be compared to James Joyce who has commented on the author's role in the narrative:

> A novelist can remain like the God of the creation, beyond his handiwork, paring his fingernails—and at the same time get his views across by allowing his characters moments of revelation in which they transcend themselves and see into the truth of things.[16]

To bring about the course of the narrative dialectically, Virginia Woolf has to take the aid of various devices. Symbolism gives us direct access to the novelist's mind, depicting exactly what thoughts or moods or feelings she wants to convey. *The Voyage Out* symbolized the author's initial attempt at fiction and the protagonist's maiden voyage into the ocean of life and society; *Night and Day* denotes the protagonist's encounter with illusion and reality.

The cognitive processes of the author are the distinctive ways of her thinking about the world, moulding her thought-processes and schematizing it consciously, inculcating her ideas and feelings into the narrative. This is where symbols are vital for transmitting the thoughts onto paper with minimum mutation of the actual feelings. The aspects which help the author in transmitting and creating his own consciousness are his perception and imagination, language being the primordial means of communication and one's perfect expression, lending profundity to her narrative. The tension of the two worlds of reality and imagination lend an aura of indecision and suspense to the story which is the integral part of an artistic mentality. Katharine Hilbery is the projection of one aspect of Virginia Woolf's personality. *Night and Day* is a deeper perspective of life as she had written it after gaining considerable experience in her married life. Naturally Katharine has a greater hold on life than Rachel. Like Mrs. Woolf, Katharine was a visionary and was never wholly involved with the external world. Her meeting with Ralph Denham puts her on guard, suspecting him to be hostile and malicious. Therefore, her grave and resolute behaviour is only a defence-mechanism to protect her sensitive being from the onslaughts of society.

Literature held no fascination for Katharine since she wanted to free herself from the shackles of her past, having spent ten precious years of her youth helping her mother to produce a biography of her grandfather. She was not as loquacious as her mother and preferred silence and solitude, fantasizing in the vast expanse of her mind about "taming of wild ponies upon the American prairies, or the conduct of a vast ship in a hurricane round a black promontory of rock." (40)

Another facet of her personality which is diagonally opposite to an illusory life was Mathematics:

> she would rather have confessed her wildest dreams of hurricane and prairie than the fact that, upstairs, alone in her room, she rose early . . . or sat up late at night to . . . work at mathematics. No force on earth would have made her confess that. (40)

The secret is the pivot around which revolves her inner being. A woman indulging in Science, Mathematics or Astronomy was unthinkable, and yet facts and figures fascinated her. Thus, we see her leading a dual existence of her real love for facts and figures and her outer involvement with literature and society. She is presented to us presiding over the tea-table but her mind is aloof and she is emotionally uninvolved.

The two people closely related to Katharine are her parents Mr. and Mrs. Hilbery. Ironically, neither of them has any cognition of their daughter's personality and temperament, nor has any similar traits. Thus the three contrary personalities are living under a single roof. Mrs. Hilbery's fascination with Shakespeare is reflected in a number of characters in the novel. This conventional love story is based on Shakespearean comedy with its initial mix-up and inevitable reunion of the lovers. The motif of Mrs. Hilbery's worshipful attitude for the great artist creeps in on personal levels:

> Your father's Hamlet, come to years of discretion; and I'm—well, I'm bit of them all, I'm quite a large bit of the fool, but the fools in Shakespeare say all the clever things. (277)

Mrs. Hilbery's external characteristics are deceptive, her charm, loquacity and vivaciousness being a cover for a strong and sensible character. But her glorious parentage sublimates all around her, especially Katharine. Katharine's greatest source of frustration was encouraging her mother to finish the biography of her grandfather.

Superficial facts are never considered very seriously by Virginia Woolf. What matters is the subconscious, the mountainous terrain of imperceptible thought-processes to be sorted out and analyzed. These will give meaning to our external actions and it is from this inner sanctum that the fountains of thought-processes are realized and the ambiguous complexities are deciphered. Katharine's domestic existence catering to the social norms is contrary to the labyrinthine processes of her world of consciousness.

William Rodney is a formal student of Shakespeare and he is portrayed as a typical masculine species, with a strain of mythopoetic tendency intertwined somewhere within his being. His poems reveal this artistic trait but he was deluged with superficialities like metre etc., submerging the actual feeling to be conveyed. For him, metre conveyed the mood but Katharine was not impressed. Shakespeare did not fascinate her, nor did she desire to experience a chill stupor on hearing it. She respected his scholarly ways but did not love him. He was alive to the conventions of society, especially regarding women. His idea was that a woman was half alive without marriage. (59) These patriarchal streaks in him placed fetters on Katharine's mind and she considered him to be "half poet and half old maid." (60) Katharine was disillusioned because her parents fell short of her vision. Her ambivalent nature alienates her from her parents as she could communicate with them only with a fraction of her self. Silence and solitude are the two notes of comfort in the life of a mystic. This is how they find solace, communing peacefully in their own worlds of consciousness. Her mother had the desired effect of arousing her feelings, but her reciprocation was slow due to the nature of her father, putting her out of gear. This struggle for the survival of her individual self resulted in her engagement to Rodney.

The dark dreary scene of the city at night is like a scene within her being, a chaotic, undefinable state, desiring a ray of understanding to illuminate the dark crevices within. People like Rodney repelled her finer instincts and she desired that no one in the world would think of her. (107) Being a true son of the patriarchy, Rodney could not penetrate the superficial barriers and unite with the sensitive vision within. Thus, imprisoned emotions of frustration were expressed maybe by actions like releasing the window shade with a snap.

Virginia Woolf has handled her protagonist very gently, like an object of art where Rodney's crudity was juxtaposed with the infinitely romantic character of Ralph Denham. As Jean Guiguet writes:

> the traditional limitations of human beings were of no importance to Virginia Woolf, and she transgresses the limits of the mind and body. She stresses that human consciousness can dilate through space to integrate, by degrees, a whole town, a whole country.[17]

Psychological hermaphroditism is a term coined by Adler wherein he described an individual who has submissive (feminine) as well as aggressive (masculine) traits. Virginia Woolf advocated this theory for a psychologically complete being which is a union of masculine and feminine characteristic traits. Ralph and Katharine are perfect examples of her idea of a complete personality. Ralph Denham is an individual with an ambivalent personality with the artistic self, which was bound firmly by his social responsibilities, struggling for release. This persistent sense of frustration fills his personality but outwardly he adopts an arrogant and domineering attitude. Being the sole earning member of his large family, he was destined to lead an impersonal life in the legal and sordid atmosphere of the solicitor's office. Once he got respite for the day from these desultory premises, he flew to the solace of his dream world of fantasy and illusion, the conscious world of his literal being. His heartfelt desire was to write a book, "In these dreams . . . he figured in noble and romantic parts." (29) Psychologically, he attempted to elevate himself from the degrading shabby conditions of his home and office, by diverting himself to other subjects like Botany or the breeding of Bull dogs. Thus we are aware of a personality whose life was perfectly organized between his two worlds of consciousness. His personal reality was envisioned in strange voyages, allowing the spirit inside him to be released because it has nothing in common with the mercenary selfish world outside. He believed in his vision's fulfilment of flowering waste tracts of earth. It was an all-consuming all-pervasive form, but he had brought the spirit under control. In his office, he radiated a feeling of self-sufficiency and an uncompromising attitude, thus making himself unpopular. His contemporaries were aliens to him in a despicable sphere of existence. Mary Datchet and his sister Joan were the two individuals he communicated with. In the very first chapter we witness the clash of two personalities—those of Katharine and Ralph. Katharine's luxurious, artistic background inspired his artistic sensibility and this anger goaded him to behave superciliously to his hostess. Katharine too was made conscious of her literary heritage. His arrogance put her on the defensive. To counteract his tennagent behaviour, Katharine appealed to his fine sensibility and he thought, "She'll do. . . . Yes, Katharine Hilbery'll do. . . . I'll take Katharine Hilbery." (21) We can understand Ralph's desperate bid to cling on to any artistic factor to help in the evolution of his own spiritual need. Overtly we get an impression of a streak of patriarchal dominance in his willingness to accept her but it is more a psychological need which Ralph is reaching out to, in the personality of Katharine. This conflict of Ralph was also Katharine's problem but this would come out in the open only in the final section of the novel where they look at one another with complete understanding.

The key figure of the narrative is Mary Datchet whose understanding and stoical acceptance of facts ensured a harmonious finale. She is an embodiment of rationality endowed with an integrated personality, not torn between two worlds of consciousness. The mythopoetic element did creep in at one stage but she did not deviate to illogical thoughts and actions, even when in love. "If love is a devastating fire which melts the whole being into one mountain torrent," (123) then neither of them is in love with the other. Extreme exhibition occurs only when the power to resist has been eaten away.

She is a happy individual, comfortably absorbed in her work. Even if her mind tends to stray away on the personal level, she shifts back to her social work of drawing the attention of eminent people and demanding the right for women to vote. In the suffragette office, we meet Sally Seal who is a disorderly character but an ardent feminist. The two intertwined crucifixes on a gold chain depict her confused state of mind. She sends clippings to her friends, exhibiting a streak of the mythopoetic tendency. The author describes her like the shadow-people, flitting in and out of the ranks of the luring eccentrics, undeveloped human beings, from whose substance some essential part had been cut away. (279) She is a dedicated suffragette, wishing to bring all the people of Russell Square and Southampton Row and speak to them about women's emancipation so that they realize the derogatory treatment meted out to women. She resembles Miss La Trobe in *Between the Acts,* a novel revolving round the vision which she attempted to project to escape momentarily from life's problems through her historical pageant. Katharine's mode of escape from this world was Mathematics and that of Denham his fantasies. Virginia Woolf very considerately deployed escape routes for the concealed emotions of her protagonists. Personally, she too required a certain occupation which lay at variance with her routine existence. Even as a child of thirteen, she used to bring out a newspaper called Hyde Park Gate. Subjugation of women was one aspect she vehemently satirized in her work, mainly because she did not believe in publicly clamouring for social reforms.

In *A Room of One's Own* too, Virginia Woolf lashes out at the subservient position of women. Her theory was that women, instead of emulating men, should further their own roles in society by "the renewal of creative power . . . to bring out and fortify the differences rather than the similarities." (87)

Formal education was denied to the protagonists of Virginia Woolf's novels. In *The Voyage Out,* Rachel's education consisted of the "rudiments of about ten branches of knowledge." (31) In *Night and Day,* Cassandra's education was "In short strands of different accomplishments." (361) Katharine desperately hides her talent at Mathematics as she is "a member of a very great profession which has, as yet, no title and very little recognition. . . . She lived at home." (40)

From 1905 to 1914, there was a new militancy in the suffragette movement. Showalter points out that Elizabeth Robin's *Votes for Women,* retitled *The Convert,* was a worthy contribution to the suffrage literature. In the great demonstration of June 1910, over a hundred women writers marched behind the 'Scrivener's banner' with Olive Schreiner, Sarah Grand, Gertrude Warden, Mary Sinclair, Mrs. Havelock Ellis and Evelyn Sharp. The Fabian Society, of which Virginia Woolf was a member, took up the question of the vote.[18]

Katharine's main conflict was about the compromise between her real self and society:

> Why . . . should there be this perpetual disparity between the life of solitude and the life of society, this astonishing precipice on one side of which the soul was active and in broad day light, on the other side of which it was contemplative and dark as night? Was it not possible to step from one to the other, erect, and without essential change? (306)

It was at this juncture of uncertainty and doubt that her relationship with Ralph took a positive turn. Katharine and Ralph have common problems regarding subjective-objective reality. Therefore, we find them vacillating between the two worlds of consciousness. They desperately try to retain their individuality and shun the mask held out to them by society. Katharine is pressurized to discard her theoretical passion and her dreams which are the purest form of her individuality. Josephine Schaefer opines: "Identical with individualized and heightened human consciousness, there is a need to liberate an individual from the constraint of the real world, that is, from the constraint of the social world which impinges upon her feelings and her own natural tendencies."[19]

Ralph, in his very first meeting with Katharine, builds up an illusory image and promptly falls in love with it. His confusion increases due to his inability to differentiate from his worlds of reality and illusion, both being variegated and separate. Katharine inspires his fantasies, and he begins to have doubts regarding reality. When he gets emotionally involved with her, his consciousness overflows the boundaries of the mind and pervades his routine earthly existence. Everything appears elevated from the inanities of this desultory life:

> The illusion of her presence became more and more complete. They seemed to pass in and out of each other's minds, questioning and answering. (401)

Virginia Woolf characterizes Ralph in a structured manner, reminding us of Bernard's artistic personality. Thus Winifred Holtby detects "two streams of thoughts—one poetical, controversial, analytical, the other creative, poetical, audacious."[20]

James Joyce envisioned infinitely more depth in an individual's inner life than in his external life. This vision he attempted to capture by way of symbols and experiences. Virginia Woolf went a step higher in voicing these ideas, woven with her inimitable language and intuitive soul. *Night and Day* and *The Voyage Out* are her own accounts of personal experiences of married life. There is a distinctive biographical element in the novel. Thus just as Leonard Woolf takes Virginia Woolf to Putney to meet his parents, Ralph takes Katharine to Highgate to meet his family. Virginia Woolf's broken engagement to Lytton Strachey is similar to Katharine's disrupted relationship to Rodney: "spiritually there was certainly no human being with whom she could claim comradeship." (256)

Virginia Woolf's relationship with men was another source of stress for her. At the time when she could have developed healthy relationship with the opposite sex, she lost both her father and her brother Thoby. In Katharine's life, the rational, intellectual element was substituted by Mathematics. Katharine's and Ralph's relationship is very delicate, like that of Virginia Woolf and Leonard Woolf. Roger Poole has concisely charted out the points of disharmony in the lives of the Woolfs—she being sensitive and aristocratic and he being rational and an intellectual. He abhorred G.E. Moore's *Principia Ethica* and it was virtually Virginia Woolf's Bible.

Katharine's engagement to Rodney proved to be a mistake for both of them. She had accepted her alienation but with his insensitive attitude, he would pull asunder her two worlds of consciousness "upon a mind bereft of all defences and keenly conscious . . . of her loneliness, of life's futility, of the barren prose of reality, of William Rodney, of her mother, and the unfinished book." (398)

Solitude and silence are the two aspects which Virginia Woolf's women find peace in, as we also notice in Dorothy Richardson's portraiture: "Loneliness, that had long gone from her life, had come back for this sudden voyaging, to be her best companion, to shelter strangeness that can only be known in solitude."[21]

For Miriam Henderson of Dorothy Richardson's *Pilgrimage*, the greatest realization of life comes only when she is alone in the presence of reality. The dictum of the Existentialists is that the individual suffers death in excessive social contact, but that this is preserved and deepened in solitude; the protagonists of Virginia Woolf's novels also experience a pilgrimage of the soul when they identify themselves with nature, being of the green-world archetype wherein their consciousness can thrive in solitude. Even in Wordsworth's *The Prelude* and *The Solitary Reaper*, we notice that his mysticism gains profundity in nature. When she is at the countryside under a starlit sky, Katharine realizes that she does not love Rodney. Similarly, Rachel discovers her feelings for Hewet in the jungles of the Amazon, similar to Robert Bridges's mind in *The Testament of Beauty* which was awakened to a "fresh initiation of life" by nature: "the domination of nature's secret urge, and happy escape therein."[22]

Pervaded with sorrow at Katharine's impending marriage, Ralph accompanies Mary to Disham to spend Christmas. A passage from *Measure for Measure* spells his gloom: "To be imprison'd in the viewless winds and blown with restless violence round about the pedant worlds." (145) On the rebound he offers marriage to Mary Datchet. Mary turns down his proposal of marriage, sensing his love for Katharine. But for a moment Mary "wound her ivy spray round the ash plant . . . but surrendered herself to complete happiness." (203)

How beautifully the author juxtaposes joy and sorrow, life and death, in that tiny action of Mary! Virginia Woolf at this juncture portrayed two simultaneous lines of action; Katharine had decided to call off the engagement and Ralph was trying really hard to forget his love for Katharine. Mary too decided to accept the truth without any bitterness and one day she disclosed to Katharine the whole truth, including Ralph's love for her. The inherent mysticism in Ralph lends a visionary appeal to Katharine. She is more a form of light to him than a human being. She is likened to music, when he sees her walking down the Strand pervading the atmosphere with order and purpose as music unifies all. While taking a walk with him, Katharine was suddenly filled with an intense realism:

> It seemed to her the immense riddle was answered, the problem had been solved. She held in her hands for one brief moment the globe which we spend our lives in trying to shape, round, whole, and entire from the confusion of chaos. (121)

In this single epiphanous moment, her life was transcended from the chaos-ridden world, to one of serenity and fulfilment. She derived certain meaning from the mass of meaninglessness surrounding her. Her life appeared to be whole and not transitory. To experience such moments of intense realism is a mystic's final desire.

Structural reliance is made on some key scenes of revelation, each character's epiphanous moment of realization of being either in love or out of love. These constitute the turning points of the narration because this love story was initially juxtaposed with incongruous characters. Virginia Woolf's moments of vision were her personal instances of life's momentary revelations. Many of her characters were endowed with this visionary gift. She was familiar with the works of all great writers and her vast storehouse of knowledge was reflected in her works. For example, a line from Dostoevsky's *The Idiots* is quoted by Katharine in one of her moments of solitude: "It is the process of discovering not the discovery itself at all." (121)

Katharine's disgust was profound in her relationship with Rodney:

> She was in one of those moods . . . of contemptible baseness, so that the necessity of association is degrading, and the tie, which at such moments is always extremely close, drags like a halter round the neck, William's exacting demands and his jealousy had pulled her down into some horrible swamp of her nature where the primeval struggle between man and woman still rages. (335)

Rodney had confessed his love for Cassandra Otway. Katharine, though in a state of shock, was willing to help him out. But his nasty behaviour is apparently in bad taste, as we gauge from Katharine's thoughts. In his company, her individuality was submerged by his vain egoistic self. But Virginia Woolf now made the stage free for Ralph though ironically he was not aware of these proceedings. When Ralph and Katharine met in Kew Gardens, her loneliness vanished due to his wonderfully interesting talk on Botany. He offered his terms of friendship wherein perfect sincerity is possible if an individual is free, with no obligation on either side. He differentiates between the two worlds of consciousness, the independent private world and the social world. Katharine continues her visions of nights, stars and moon but they become associated with her subconscious love for Ralph: "she had committed no sacrilege, but enriched herself, perhaps immeasurably, perhaps eternally, she hardly dared steep herself in the infinite bliss." (522)

David Daiches is of the opinion that engagements and marriages are symbols of emotional adjustment in this discrete and disparate world. This alignment of two individuals depicts a thematic solution to the disparities enshrouding our lives. Jean Guiguet feels that the exchange of partners is only each person resisting social demands and emphasizing his individuality by way of thoughts and emotions.[23]

Love is an important factor for self-realization, a turn of the mind which strengthens relationships broadening one's perspective: "To seek a true feeling among the chaos of the unfeelings or half-feelings of life, to recognize it when found and to accept the consequences of the discovery." (358)

This is the stepping stone to our survival in society. If an individual can accept one person as part of herself, then she will steadily coexist with other individuals on different levels of relationships. Therefore, love and marriage play a pivotal role for a person who feels alienated from society surrounded subconsciously by unbridgeable abysses. The million-dollar question is whether one can find an individual for a complete harmonious relationship.

Katharine attempts to dissuade Ralph from loving her because it was only illusory. Finally, to communicate freely, Katharine perceived his vision of reality through the symbolic dot surrounded by little flames. The letter turns itself into a drawing, the only expression, he can find for his idea: a 'little dot' with 'flames' round it. Katharine answers in the affirmative. "Yes, the world looks something like that to me too." (458) Ralph discovered her love for Mathematics too and this led to their being united in a mystical silence which no force could tear asunder. They would face life together sharing the impending future, with its vast impenetrable mysteries, silently adoring each other. Her frail beam of truth had been united with another soul who was also a visionary and a mystical being.

The final reunion of the lovers is made by the flower-laden Mrs. Hilbery who had just returned from Shakespeare's tomb. Her ritual role as sanctifier resembles the fertility myth in T.S. Eliot's *The Waste Land.* Mrs. Milvain's reprisal at the activities of the youngsters disgusted Katharine but realization hits her when she views the happenings from her aunt's angle of vision and she realizes "how infinitely repulsive the body of life is without its soul." (431)

So we are back to the consciousness of Katharine, her empathy with her personal way of living, and the distaste of social existence, the outer shell represented by our bodies. This ambivalent nature describing solitude and groupism leads to a streak of instability in her personality. Her desisting and hesitant behaviour is misinterpreted and her relationships tend to get away from society. She was transfused with joy by the jugglery of numerals but it was science and thus, being born a woman, she had to hide it from society. But when Ralph treads on this *sanctum sanctorum* of her inner being, "she looked like a wild bird just settling with wings trembling to fold themselves—the moment of exposure had been extremely painful." (446) In Ralph's company her silence and desire for solitude would always be respected.

The reader is able to feel the process and experience the intimacy of the character in the book. The more we feel the process, the greater our involvement with the character. We perceive the depth of the problems regarding love, marriage and solitude required for harmonious existence. Holtby points out that in the conclusion of *Night and Day,* "the dream would become identified with reality, the night changed into day, the union was complete, a union not so much of a man with a woman, as of a man with himself, a woman with herself."[24]

There is therefore a progress: where Rachel of *The Voyage Out* fails, Katharine of *Night and Day* triumphs. Her individuality remains sacred to her and continues to be on the pedestal where she had always kept it. Thus, Katharine, unlike Rachel, emerges all the more a confident individual, willing to face life and society with Ralph as her companion. Their friendship has been established in the higher realm of life, unperceived by anyone, in a realm of independence, understanding and love. They will be in a perpetual search delving into each other's personalities in the hope of discovering a nugget of truth and renewing their relationship over and over again.

NOTES

1. Mitchell A. Leaska, *The Novels of Virginia Woolf: From Beginning to End* (London: Weidenfield and Nicolson, 1977), p. 12.
2. L. Woolf and James Strachey, ed., *Virginia Woolf and Lytton Strachey: Letters* (London: The Hogarth Press, 1956), p. 75.
3. Virginia Woolf, *The Voyage Out* (London: The Hogarth Press, 1915), p. 206.
4. Jean-Paul Sartre, *Being and Nothingness,* trans. Hazel E. Barnes (London: Methuen, 1957), p. 252.
5. Jean Guiguet, *Virginia Woolf and Her Works*, trans. Jean Stewart (London: The Hogarth Press, 1965), p. 197.
6. William James, *Psychology: The Briefer Course*, quoted from *Classic and Contemporary Perspectives,* ed. Chad Gordon and Kenneth J. Gergen (New York: John Wiley, 1968), pp. 42-43
7. Winifred Holtby, *Virginia Woolf* (London: Wishart, 1932), p. 62.
8. Ernest Keen, p. 43.
9. Jean O. Love, *Worlds in Consciousness: The Mythopoetic Thought in the Novels of Virginia Woolf* (Berkeley: University of California Press, 1970), pp. 105-106.
10. Weigert, ed., "Existentialism and Its Relation to Psychotheraphy," *Psychiatry*, Vol. 12, No. 4, November, 1949, Text 226, p. 405.
11. Virginia Woolf, *Night and Day* (London: The Hogarth Press, 1919), p. 470.
12. Carol H. Mackay, *"The Thackeray Connection"* in Jane Marcus, ed., p. 76.
13. Charlotte Bronte, *Jane Eyre* (New York: Collier Books, 1962), p. 119.

14. Virginia Woolf, *A Room of One's Own* (New York: The Hogarth Press, 1929), p. 47.
15. *A Writer's Diary*, 27th March, 1919, p. 10.
16. James Joyce, *A Portrait of the Artist as a Young Man*, quoted from Morris Beja, *Epiphany in the Modern Novel: Revelation as an Art* (Seattle: University of Washington Press, 1971), p. 237.
17. Jean Guiguet, p. 37.
18. Elaine Showalter, *A Literature of Their Own: British Women Novelists from Bronte to Lessing* (Princeton: Princeton University Press, 1977), p. 218.
19. Josephine O'Brien Schaefer, *The Three-Fold Nature of Reality* (The Hague: Mouton, 1965), p. 50.
20. Winifred Holtby, p. 200
21. Dorothy Richardson, *Pilgrimage* (London: Dent, 1938), IV, p. 24.
22. Robert Bridges, *The Testament of Beauty* (New York: Oxford University Press, 1929), pp. 44-45.
23. Jean Guiguet, p. 208.
24. Winifred Holtby, p. 93.

The Edge of Consciousness

Virginia Woolf's deviation from the traditional narrative technique was established with the publication of *Jacob's Room* in 1922, the year when James Joyce published his *Ulysses*, T.S. Eliot *The Waste Land* and Franz Kafka *The Trial.* After *Night and Day,* Virginia Woolf's essay on "Modern Fiction" gave the blueprint for an original form of narration. In 1920 she wrote in her diary that she desired to adopt a wholly new technique, completely different from the traditional track of *The Voyage Out* and *Night and Day:*

> Having this afternoon arrived at some idea of a new form for a new novel. Suppose one thing should open out of another . . . as in *An Unwritten Novel*--only not for ten pages but two hundred or so—doesn't that give the looseness and tightness I want; doesn't that get closer and yet keep form and speed, and enclose everything, everything. My doubt is how far it will enclose the human heart—Am I sufficiently mistress of my dialogue to net it there? For I figure that the approach will be entirely different this time; no scaffolding; scarcely a brick to be seen; all crepuscular, but the heart, the passion, humour, everything as bright as fire in the mist. Then I'll find room for so much—a gaiety—an inconsequence—a light-spirited stepping at my sweet will. Whether I'm sufficiently mistress of thing—that's the doubt; but conceive *Mark on the Wall, Kew Garden* and *An Unwritten Novel,* taking hands and dancing in unity. What the unity shall be I have yet to discover, the theme is blank to me.[1]

Hermione Lee writes that *Jacob's Room* suggests the room of the universe into which he is merged and it is also the book itself.[2] Jacob's contribution to society was his attitudes and feelings which were the controlling factors of his interaction with the world. This life space was his room, his area of living and our spatial knowledge of it, which denotes the title.

Jacob's Room is the narration of man's life from a multiple point of view, apparently an extension of the Bildungsroman. Virginia Woolf has adopted a discontinuous technique of severing the individual growth of a young man by the First World War. *A Portrait of the Artist as a Young Man* also presents a similar viewpoint. Virginia Woolf projects her horror for modern warfare which is the mechanism that destroys the fragile tender seed of man's individuality impeding his complete transaction with society. She delineates the characteristics of her protagonists, on the basis of psychological realism adopting a technique where a sprinkling of ideas and feelings is the main basis for the description. In such novels, the traditional and direct narratives are of no consequence. The author traces the life of an individual by his experiences, the steady unfurling of his consciousness, his identification with life and its joys and sorrows, and the little impression which means so much to the world of the sensitive that go unnoticed by the materialistic Jacob's sensitivity and his intense desire for individuality makes him refuse to accept the world's follies. It is not a traditional narrative but a string of thoughts and ideas being focussed on Jacob. Therefore, to have dialectically projected these ideas was an impossibility. Fragmentary thoughts are strewn all over and no unity prevails. At Cambridge, a group of students discuss a spiritual topic but everything remains at a standstill and with the disintegration of the group, letters are the only thread which is continuously woven through the narrative:

> to see one's own envelope on another's table is to realize how soon deeds sever and become alien. Then at last the power of the mind to quit the body is manifest, and perhaps we fear or hate or wish annihilated this phantom of ourselves, lying on

the table.[3]

The unusual technique adopted by Virginia Woolf in *Jacob's Room* is necessary for the expression of her portrayal of the elusive quality in human nature, the individual's consciousness and the projection of that spirit which can possess a degree of imagination and sensitivity. There is not much utilization of the stream-of-consciousness technique and there is no trace of a plot. We are given a peep into life, a poetic unravelling of normal existence. She ends the book with Bonamy's cry of anguish for Jacob as she had commenced the novel with the tears of Betty Flanders due to uncertainty and insecurity. As the book proceeds, we try to gauge a complete pattern, the true life impression, which Virginia Woolf attempts to convey to us. What she has chosen to express in words cannot be fulfilled through mere narration but by various techniques of juxtaposition and sequential portrayal. By the little hints very subtly given, we can delve into the deeper strata of her mind which she is attempting to present: "It is no use trying to sum people up. One must follow hints, not exactly what is said, nor yet entirely what is done." (29)

We have a glimpse of Virginia Woolf's technique on the very first page of the novel. We get acquainted with Betty Flanders and through her eyes we read her letter and the surroundings. Her tears distort her vision, conveying the vulnerable position she emotionally is in. Omniscient narration projects the background with mere hints and flashbacks. The slender threads of narration branch out through metaphorical and symbolical aids, weaving a fabric intricately patterned.

This is a shadowy, complex and indirect portrayal, requiring a different tone and style of narration, sufficiently flexible to incorporate her new trend, fusing experiment and presentation of true reality with biographical fragments:

> One such belief is that the individual in his daily life is cut off from "reality" but at rare moments receives a shock. These shocks or "moments of being" are not, as she had imagined

as a child, simply random manifestation of some malevolent force but "a token of some real thing behind appearances." The idea of a privileged moment when a spiritually transcendent truth of either personal or cosmic dimension is perceived in a flash of intuition is, of course, a commonplace of religious experience and in particular of mystical traditions of thought as well as a recurrent feature of idealist philosophies from Plato onwards.[4]

The novel is a series of sketches of Jacob's childhood and youth, a projection of various impressions of the individuals and their consciousness forming the different motifs of the narration. Externally, the novel is founded on a sequential basis of portraying the crucial stages of Jacob's life. A couple of impressions are given to inform us about his parents, Seabrook and Betty Flanders. At one stage we see him collecting butterflies at Scarborough. Then he is shown to be a Cambridge student. Next he is visualized holidaying at Cornwall with his friend Timothy Durrant. We are given a view of his life in London and his friendship with Florinda. We witness the initiation of his career and his affair with Florinda. He then develops good relations with Bonamy. Fanny Elmer's infatuation with Jacob is mentioned. We experience his brief Bohemian Paris visit which was extended to Italy and Greece where he fell in love with Sandra Wentworth Williams. He returns to England just before the declaration of the First World War and finally his death in combat. Virginia Woolf deviated from the traditional norms to a lyrical style which lends a mythopoetic aura to the narrative. Her inner thoughts and feelings frame the quotidian theme into an extraordinarily beautiful rendering, projecting the hidden depths and beauty of her inner being which was enshrouded in a mystical halo. The death of the individual is stressed by her artistic portraiture which is the secret of evolving those intricate feelings to the surface. It is with perfect character-schematization that Virginia Woolf projects the interrelated aspects bringing into view two major events in man's existence which are life and death. She also focuses on Jacob's interaction with women and his literary knowledge which was the patriarchal birthright of a male.

Jacob does not indulge much in reflection and therefore there are not many transferences between the past and the present. Time is a temporary phase, transient, upholding a momentary happening. As a result all experiences are imbued into timelessness. Mr. Floyd had become the principal of Maresfield House and had seen Jacob as a little boy in Scarborough. In a single sentence, Jacob had grown into a fine young man whom Mr. Floyd recognized "after three seconds." (20) In a single sentence and within a short span of time, a relationship was established, past and present were intermingled. The learned men of the past had heard the chimes and released them time-worn, to the present generation. Jacob stood at his window, serenely listening to the chimes of the clock: "He looked satisfied; indeed masterly." (42) Present time depicted by the clock and the past represented by the legends on the tombstone are very well juxtaposed. Epistolatory method too brings about temporal and spatial unity. Jacob writes to his mother from Paris and we are informed of his departure. Then he writes from Italy and time passes with the Church Clock.

Jacob's three rooms in his Cornish cottage, Cambridge and in London signify the process of his growth as an individual, his interest in nature which diversifies to literature and finally his involvement in the Greek way of life. The room image is developed from the first novel *The Voyage Out* wherein Rachel visits people in their rooms which are "apt to give off something of the same shock as their faces when seen for the first time." (203) Miss Allan's room had "balm for all anguish." (312) After Rachel's death, her friends have suddenly the keen feeling of "someone's personality, she felt Rachel in the room with her." (444) The indication of Jacob's extra-corporeal presence in his room after his death is given by the creaking of his wicker chair. Ralph Denham in *Night and Day* gauges Katharine by her aristocratic room but it is in his shabby room that he unites with Katharine in his fantasy, "the utmost fullness of communion seemed to be there." (409) Virginia Woolf projected the image of the Bloomsbury Group in the form of the informal literary gatherings in Mary Datchet's room.

Virginia Woolf has stressed a considerable amount of literature which Jacob was interested in. While describing his room Virginia Woolf acquaints us with Jacob's interest in Elizabethan and Greek literature. Jacob's death is implied by the pressed poppies in the Greek dictionary. This description might have a biographical undertone as Virginia Woolf's brother Thoby had died after being infected with typhoid during a holiday in Greece.

Jacob's ambiguous nature is juxtaposed with his experience of society. His other aspects of cultural education are presented by various references, one of which is the British Museum wherein all the literary giants are placed under a single roof:

> There is in the British Museum an enormous mind. Consider that Plato is there cheek by jowl with Aristotle; and Shakespeare with Marlowe. . . . The *Phaedrus* is very difficult. . . . The dialogue draws to its close. . . . Plato's argument is stowed away in Jacob's mind and for five minutes Jacob's mind continues alone, onwards, into the darkness. (107-9)

Jacob's identification with nature is described by his constant fascination for moths and butterflies. The novel is pervaded by insects and their various descriptions and many a time Jacob's day-dreams figure round a tree: "a tree had fallen on a windless night and th . red underwing had circled round the lantern and flown away, never to return." (22)

> The moth image which the author so beautifully projected, is thematic, when considered deeply. It was as if someone had taken a tiny bead of pure life and decking it as lightly as possible with down and feathers, had set it dancing and zigzagging to show us the true nature of life. Thus displayed one could not get over the strangeness of it. One is apt to forget all about life. . . . The insignificant little creature now knew death. As I looked at the dead moth, this minute wayside triumph of so great a force over so mean an antagonist filled

> me with wonder. Just as life has been strange a few minutes before, so death was now as strange. The moth having righted himself now lay most decently and uncomplainingly composed. O yes, he seemed to say, death is stronger than I am.[5]

This novel is prevalent with imagery, a juxtaposition of sounds and rhythms of the caressing rivers and the colourful inhabitants of nature focussed in their natural habitat. On reading, we are immured by a peaceful rendition of the influence of an individual's personality by nature, knowledge, society and his own self. The emotional response of the reader is assured by Virginia Woolf's beautiful imagery which when considered finally is like a flower blooming, the grand finale of simultaneous portrayals of natural objects which will be the final revelation of her message.

The wind and sea imagery are utilized to unite the whole narration weaving motifs of the individual and society. The Greek Sea imagery was presented by the Scarborough and Cornwall experiences which finally decimate into Jacob's travels and his death. Jacob's character is schematized mainly with dexterous applications of imagery.

Jacob is an impenetrable personality and we are to gauge him by the few impressions we gather about him from the novel. He is as elusive as the wind and a wild horse, very subtly attempting to establish his individuality. His physical aspects are shown all over the book like the petals of a flower. This ambiguity leaves us in suspense and like the iceberg it is for us to gauge his psychological depth and realism.

Tindall in *The Literary Symbol* gives a sketchy description of Kafka's *The Castle*, the hero's efforts and frustrations, enhancing the central image and all the characters connected with the castle. This great image, like Virginia Woolf's Parthenon and lighthouse imagery, embodies total reality—sociological, psychological and religious. Man's loneliness, his aspirations and his desire to know what he cannot know are portrayed by Kafka. *The Castle* reveals man's confrontation with the universe as does *Moby Dick*.[6] Similarly, Jacob clashes with society to realize his own sense of reality which eludes him.

Jacob's mother Betty Flanders has been a widow for two years and she is introduced on the opening page in the act of writing a letter. She is emotionally perturbed because she is anxious about Jacob's whereabouts. She was writing to Captain Barfoot who was a family friend. Along with the progress of the letter we are informed about her three sons, Jacob, Archer and a baby in a perambulator. Her tears interconnect her past and present but we are not given the cause of this emotional upheaval. Mrs. Flanders's presence in the novel emanates a feeling of permanence and stability, something constructive to cling on to in this flowing evanescent narrative. Her actions have been depicted accurately with no poetic influences. A straightforward narrative of her external activities but no access to her mind and its intricacies. She is an extremely attractive woman, forty-five years old with tremendous physical energy. Her husband Seabrook was a man with wild habits and therefore her attraction for the sober respectable Captain. It is only through his influence that Jacob avails the opportunity of attending Cambridge. This is where he came actually into contact with society. Mr. Plumer was the Cambridge don whom Virginia Woolf has portrayed on the lines of her grandfather Sir James and her father Sir Leslie Stephen who had dual personalities which were androgynous by nature. One half was an intellectual, rational, Cambridge don, author, patriarchal Anglican Clergyman, the other half was excessively sentimental, with an absurdly self-pitying trait.

Jacob did not have much patience with Mr. Plumer as he preferred solitude. At Cambridge he met girls and boys amongst whom Timmy Durrant was his companion. They went to Sicily together but his mind was involved with only a single question:

> No doubt if this were Italy, Greece or even the shores of Spain, sadness would be routed by strangeness and excitement and the nudge of a classical education. But the Cornish hills have stark chimneys standing on them, and, somehow or other, loveliness is infernally sad. Yes, the chimneys and the

coastguard stations and the little bays with the waves breaking unseen by anyone make one remember the overpowering sorrow. And what can this sorrow be? (56)

Virginia Woolf has portrayed Jacob's hidden depths in this beautiful passage. His real self was like the chimney and the unseen waves were his inner being, his imperceptible sadness unperceived by anyone. He could not decipher any values even from religion. Even though the author was an agnostic she did introduce sprinklings of religion in her narrative. Mr. Charles Steele, like Lily Briscoe in *To the Lighthouse* sported a cross not in a chain but on his watch strap, something to cling to as a source of moral courage. He too was a painter and just as Lily completed her painting with a line of colour, Steele picturized Mrs. Flanders in his painting with a violet-black dot to brighten things up: "it was just that note which brought the rest together." (7) Jimmy's and Jacob's attempt to discuss religion too was pathetic. Like Steele's realistic dot of colour, they attempted to sing hymns which seemed to them the best means of communing with the Almighty:

Rock of Ages, cleft for me
Let me hide myself in Thee. (49)

Their friendly chatter was illuminated by the solemn beam of the lighthouse. Virginia Woolf's philosophy may have symbolized it as the light of God, guiding them in their life.

In the party that Florinda attends, the room is dark and everybody appears like a phantom figure. Florinda's unhappiness and her deliberate smashing of the globe is an eerie symbol. This is followed by the rest of the merrymakers crowning Jacob with flowers and placing him on a gilt chair. Florinda meanwhile was holding on to him and crying. Virginia Woolf has tried to evoke Christ's crucifixion in this scene wherein Jesus was being crowned with thorns and Mary holding on to him and weeping, with the onlookers rejoicing. Jacob like Jesus projects truth and reality which will be circumvented and annihilated by people and society at large.

Jacob's interaction with different individuals will create an inroad to self-discovery. His communication and contribution to society are what finally matter. But his mind is a fluctuating mass with nothing substantial to anchor himself to, except of course his strong belief in his individuality: "the obstinate irrepressible conviction which makes youth so intolerably disagreeable—I am what I am, and intend to be it, for which there will be no form in the world, unless Jacob makes one for himself." (159) His social identity was established firmly even at that tender age.

An individual's lifestyle, his environment, his experiences of trauma and frustration are steadily evoked in the mental processes and thus his attitude towards life will acquire negative traits. These character traits will change the very conception of life of the individual. A.H. Maslow in his well-known paper "Frustration, Threat and Deprivation," states that only "a deprivation which is at the same time a threat to the personality, that is, to the life goals of the individual to his defensive system, to his self esteem, or to his feeling of security" will have "frustrating effects."[7]

We can trace Jacob's life by his relation to society and his reaction to many incidents. Jacob is introduced in an incident where while climbing a rock he is fascinated by the appearance of a crab. But the sight of a sun-bathing couple terrorizes him and he runs towards a big rock for shelter which the terror-stricken boy presumes to be his nanny. His dislike for company is thus conveyed to the readers. Like Dorothy Richardson's *Pilgrimage* which consists of many brief sections, traversing from moment to moment, a single scene or a patch of conversation or an observation on Jacob and his lifestyle—the interrelation of those perceptions and revelations are miraculously brought about. In reality, it should appeal like the choppy sea, disintegrated ideas toppling and tumbling over one another.

Clara Durrant is introduced in a haze of colour and Jacob perceives the name in yellow gauze. While plucking grapes, he once again sees her as "semi-transparent, pale, wonderfully beautiful." (159) Then we hear not her voice but the rendition of her diary. The paper flowers and white satin shoes are symbolical of a hypocritical social existence. She resembles Katharine Hilbery leading an illusory life of catering to her mother's desires, entertaining and loving Jacob silently. Virginia Woolf has portrayed another aspect of herself which had hurt her immeasurably. Many a time, people have stopped on the road and laughed at her. Ironically society never could understand or respect an individual with a philosophical bent of mind. They are always relegated to the sanatorium or the jungles. Miss Marchmont could never resist the Elgin Marbles: "she looked at them sideways, waving her hand and muttering a word or two of salutation which made Jacob and the other man turn around. She smiled at them amiably. It all came into her philosophy—that colour is sound, or perhaps it has something to do with music." (104)

Katharine Hilbery too was seen uttering a sentence from Dostoevsky's *The Idiots* while walking down the Strand. But an idiosyncratic man will never be jeered at. Mr. Huxtable wrote letters in Greek and was familiar with science, pictures and architecture, and was also a musician. Virginia Woolf retorted by intermingling the expensive literary books with the pigeon holes meant for keeping umbrellas and walking sticks, taunting at compartmentalized knowledge, leading nowhere but creating mere pedantics. They lack aestheticism and beauty and like morons are led to the altar of knowledge, a routine, mundane affair between the great institution and their rational, intellectual inhabitants. Realism, art, beauty, the backbone of literature were missing. Jacob too with his infinite sensibility failed to discover Miss Marchmont's beauty of the soul but stared askance at her.

Bonamy loved Jacob in his own abnormal manner. His taste in literature too was in a twisted vein, preferring hard and constructed narrations to flowery, rambling literature. Many of the Bloomsbury members harboured homosexual tendencies and therefore, Virginia Woolf was free to mix with them in an uninhibited manner without any complications. Jacob thus befriended Bonamy when he had taken up a profession, just for the sake of company. During his outings with him Jacob met Florinda who was a prostitute. She was a girl with doubtful parentage. Jacob believed her to be chaste and therefore responded to her overtures of love. But in reality she was forlorn and miserable having forsaken her chastity, the only possession which she had cherished, being homeless and uneducated. Shelley would not penetrate her head and she could not even read her love letters properly. Her sentiments were infantile and she looked like a Greek, wild and frail. She was bored with this derogatory existence. Even "when the body escaped mutilation, seldom did the heart go to the grave unscarred." (76) Jacob enjoyed Florinda physically but sometimes he wondered whether she had a mind. At heart she was a religious and sincere person. Jacob looked through all the superficialities and gauged a very soothing quality in her—her inviolable fidelity. Unfortunately, he saw her the next day in the arms of another man. We deduce his optimistic nature in the cool manner he absorbs this tragic scene. His initial relationship with a woman ends in tragedy. But his philosophic nature helps him to continue living normally.

The subjective element is very well portrayed in *Jacob's Room.* As the Victorian age passes into the Edwardian, the young Stephens developed interest in different directions. Thoby went to Cambridge, Vanessa took up painting and Virginia took up writing. This was the nucleus of the Bloomsbury Group emerging from these serious truth-oriented individuals. Thoby's memory seems to have been honoured in *Jacob's Room.* Jack Hills at this stage gave them a book on *Butterflies and Moths*, the insects about whom they had studied and whom they stored in jars. Therefore the all-pervasive butterfly and moth imagery in this novel is connected with Julia's and Stella's death and had united the children in adversity though they never mentioned it: "this silence was known to cover something."[8]

Realism to Jacob was beyond his understanding. As a child, he could identify himself with nature, the rocks, the sand, the jelly fish, the sheep's skull; this continuous, changing picture of the world appealed to him and he was totally involved. He imbibed Nature and became one with it; but he could not decipher human beings nor socialize with them. Even in school when he visualized the cows and children in a field, he would get immersed, "'Jacob's Off' thought Durrant" (35) He flies from the University Professor's luncheon and seeks solitude by the river. For him, "It's not the catastrophes, murders, deaths, diseases that age and kill us; it's the way people look and laugh and run up the steps of omnibuses." (133) This is a direct recording of Virginia's own philosophy of life.

Jacob too was portrayed as a sensitive boy wherein, he feels, "words were inaudible. It was the intimacy, a sort of spiritual suppleness, which mind imprints upon mind indelibly." (44) Society impedes him and his consciousness, makes it difficult for him to survive, having to cater to social exigencies of dress and behaviour. The author reminisces of the eighteenth century lifestyle and wonders, "Each had his past shut in him like the leaves of a book known to him by heart and his friends could only read the title." (62) She attempts to protect the individuality of her protagonists and their moody, introvert behaviour which was a part of her, "if there is such a thing as a shell secreted by man to fit man himself here we find it. . . . The change of moods wears us out." (62)

Silence and solitude focus on the invisible life of an individual. Terence Hewet wanted to write a novel on silence. T.S. Eliot too was interested in silence. He wrote an unpublished poem on "Silence" in 1910, describing how while walking one day in city streets, he sees them shrink and divide. . . . His everyday preoccupations, his past, all the claims of the future are wiped out by the commanding silence. "Silence" is Eliot's first and perhaps most lucid description of the timeless moment. He concludes that there is nothing else beside it.[9]

Jacob is a highly philosophical being and therefore Florinda's despicable behaviour does not make much of an impression on him. He sometimes visualizes the body of Clara and Florinda as a transfused mass of colour. T.E. Apter compares this ethereal quality of Jacob to Dante's philosophical mind.

In the Introduction to *The Nature of Human Consciousness,* Ornstein writes on the scientific and mystical ways of knowing life:

> Those two ways of thinking, the way of time and history, and

> the way of eternity and timelessness, are both part of man's effort to comprehend the world in the other nor reducible to it . . . each supplementing the other, neither telling the whole story.[10]

Virginia Woolf in her early twenties had lived through three deaths and two of them had precipitated her into madness. Thoby's death shattered her and she failed to face the reality of it. In *Jacob's Room* and *The Waves,* she attempted to recapture him amidst his beloved Greece. Her powerful juxtapositions signified earth, very often like the sheep's skull and children collecting dead moths and beetles and also the attempt to revive Seabrook, through the waves and Church bells. Fanny Elmer is seen wending her way from the graveyard, under Jacob's window. This symbolized death being brought to Jacob, implying that death was stalking him. Avrom Fleishmen writes:

> One further aspect of the intuition of order is to be distinguished in Jacob's experience; the dualism of life and death which is crystallised in the image of a circle of light in an encompassing darkness. The sure grasp of the reality of things which comes to the butterfly collectors watching the insects emerge and which comes to the sleeper as he wakes to discover the objects, and around his room in this grasp is accompanied by a clear view of the mortality which encumbers them.[11]

At Jacob's death, everything is diffused, everything was left, "just as it was. . . . Nothing arranged." (176) Thus Virginia Woolf immortalized him and granted him eternal life. T.E. Apter has given a fitting tribute at the conclusion:

> Jacob can merely contemplate such release as he looks at a single wild red cyclamen which survives, somehow, amid the comedy of love and the tragedy of social restrictions that surround him. Jacob's strength lies in his assurance of this

possibility of independence and release, and in his sensitivity to the cruelty that is usually imperceptibly inflicted upon its members. He has, however, no strength to resist that which he understands to be opposed to him, and when he dies, a victim of war and thus of society's ignorant cruelty, it seems that there is little left of him but—as his mother finds in the confusion of his room—a pair of old boots.[12]

Jacob's death symbolizes man's fate and his death came only after he was able to impress society with his personality and individuality. Each of the rude array of characters presented were impressed and enamoured by his physical beauty and not by the infinite depths of his soul.

II

We are bound in our mental processes by memories, reactions and obsessions. As an artist, Virginia Woolf is something of a philosopher—gentle, serene, with a refined air of mysticism. Here was a centripetal trend of writing, an inward voyage, delving into the hitherto unexplored depths of the mind. This fresh perception offers us wonderful avenues for experimentation on an individual, an infinitely wider scope for a cognitive approach in this genre. Virginia Woolf's fascination for reading and criticism inspired the writer in her. The books which she read give us a glimpse of her personality. To quote a few names: Wilfred Trotter's *Instincts of the Herd in Peace and War,* Marcel Proust's *A La Recherche du Temps Perdu*, Charles Darwin's *The Origin of Species*, Friend's *Civilization and its Discontents: Moses and Monotheism.* Woolf had delved into original Greek literature which reflects the strains of classicism in her novels.

Initially, her novels were traditionalistic—*The Voyage Out* and *Night and Day.* But with *Jacob's Room,* she veered from an objective to an entirely subjective attitude and the Woolfian technique was finally established as an art form in *Mrs. Dalloway* where we are introduced to the "*tunnelling process.*" Mrs. Woolf's very own technique, the movement between present time and past experiences, is handled with perfection with the help of her innate feminine intuition. She has very cleverly adapted the subjective method, ideal for an introspective person like her. She possessed a speculative mind and along with her life's philosophy, she contributed greatly to this trend of thought. She was fascinated by Bergson and Henry James, since she could identify her thought-processes with their theories. Her novels are devoid of high-flown drama, violence or any sort of extreme activities. Her characters are the life and soul of her creations. Subjectivism was present in Milton and Shakespeare and was thus not a new phenomenon in the nineteenth century. The Durkheimian Theory is a conception of the way in which man exists in society and society is another facet of ourselves, a counterpart of our inner beings. The relation between the individual and society is based on delicate and flexible issues. The individual's responsibility towards society is counteracted by society's responsibility for the happiness and emotional security of the individual. Extreme individuation of the mind leads to loneliness and excessive socialization destroying the individual's inner life which demands a certain period of solitude.

The conciousness of every individual is woven in a suitable fabric which represents the social consciousness. An individual should simultaneously enact two roles by being a part of the objective world and also by leading an independent existence, i.e. he should be able to correlate his individual values and the universal values on a single plane for harmonious living.

In *Mrs. Dalloway,* Virginia Woolf utilizes a multifaceted narrative-technique of direct and indirect narration which absorbs us completely and illuminates the thoughts and feelings of the protagonists. As the author writes in *The Death of the Moth and Other Essays*, "a novelist's chief desire is to be as unconscious as possible . . . so that nothing may disturb or disquiet the mysterious nosing about, feeling around . . . of that very shy and elusive spirit, the imagination."[13] Virginia Woolf and James Joyce attempted a new kind of realism, an attempt to document the whole world of sensations and to capture fugitive thoughts in their progress through the mind in the very moment of their flow and convey elusive and evanescent thoughts—words that come to the mind, images of the inner world of fantasy, fusing with sounds and smells, the world of perceptual experience.[14]

In a letter to Violet Dickinson in 1903, she revealed her subconscious ideas about the novel which she was going to venture: "I'm going to have a man and a woman—show them growing up—never meeting—not knowing each other—but all the time you'll feel them coming nearer and nearer. This will be the real exciting part (as you see)."[15]

The three protagonists in *Mrs. Dalloway* are initially on different levels of consciousness—physical, complex and neutral. But this schematization diminishes when Clarissa and Septimus are diffused by their consciousness and Peter too finally reaches out to Clarissa's plane of consciousness. The narrative thus concludes on a note of a unitary whole. Jean O. Love elaborates her idea:

> Some of the rich plurisignificance of the novel, of its character and of its events as symbolic vehicles, begins to be apparent when the surface events are understood in terms of their more essential mythic order. Clarissa is more than an ordinary hostess. She has powers almost like those of some mythic goddess or great earth mother, as if she were some visible manifestation of Brahma or Mana. At the very minimum, she is the 'true believer' in preexistent unity. Septimus's insanity is not only insanity, it is also nature worship and pantheism—an ultimate but exaggerated and unbalanced communion with the cosmos. The day of the novel is not a single day; instead, it is a mythic symbol of timelessness. London is an elaborate 'room,' therefore the universe, and is also the timeless city outside space. Clarissa and Septimus are not strangers, on the level of spirit or consciousness, they and Peter are timelessly and eternally one. Septimus's death is the living out, the consummation of his desire for union with the cosmos. The party is a grand spiritual union, with and within the spirit of Clarissa, where the scales drop from all eyes and all illusions

of separateness and individuality vanish.[16]

The narration is spread out over a single day. Clarissa Dalloway, a middle-aged but sprightly London hostess, the wife of a politician, was to give a party on a day in June. She is outwardly poised and controlled but in an interior monologue we realize the regrets which she harbours in her heart. Then we meet her old suitor Peter Walsh who has just returned from India and the memories are revived. Her seventeen-year old daughter is described, followed by an account of her history-teacher Doris Kilman. Clarissa finds her obnoxious because she took up so much of Elizabeth's time and attempts to inculcate religious feelings in her. Richard appears for a time and reassures her of his love, silently, with a bunch of roses.

Simultaneously Septimus Warren Smith is portrayed in an increased state of insanity and his wife Rezia who is desperately attempting to keep him sane. Finally he commits suicide and this news is conveyed by Sir William Bradshaw at Clarissa's party. This Joycean portrayal discerns reality out of the mass of quotidian happenings. The story is woven in the leitmotif of time, with the present, past and future intermingled to integrate the narrative into a whole.

The theme of *Mrs. Dalloway* is centrally situated in a single emotion around which other associations conjoin and through this cadenced fabric of thought, we can visualize the mood of the narrative. The beauty of its lyricism is that there are no passionate outbursts or sloppy sentimentalism. Joyce's *Ulysses* made an impact on her and it is from this book that she gained an insight into solitude. This book was her major breakthrough on the innovative plane, the stream-of-consciousness technique: "It was something central which permeated, something warm which broke up surfaces and rippled the cold contact of man and woman, or of women together." (36) This sentence is a direct transcription of the consciousness, an expression of the inner meaning.

The autobiographical element in *Mrs. Dalloway* is very apparent. It is the subjective imagery which Woolf utilized in every vein of her narrative. Almost all the characters have in reality been known to her because they can be identified with people whom she had known in her own life. This we learn from the biographical works about her written by Quentin Bell and Aileen Pippet, from the writings of Leonard Woolf and from Virginia's own diary. These aspects are interwoven as the essay proceeds. So far as time is concerned, Virginia Woolf has practically utilized Bergson's theory of inner time and outer time. Physical time, which is indicated by the clock, is impersonal. Thus:

> It was precisely twelve O'clock, twelve by Big Ben; whose stroke was wafted through the Northern part of London; blent with that of other clocks, mixed in a thin ethereal way with the clouds and wisps of smoke and died up among the seagulls. (104)

The sound of Big Ben is an unifying aspect throughout the book. It is an empirical-theoretical device in a purely mythopoetic narrative. But it is an essential element to guide it punctually through the restricted period of activity. As the Big Ben unifies Clarissa's consciousness, so does St. Margaret diffuse Clarissa with Peter's being, because he felt that its "life-like ringing—which wants to confide itself, with a tremor of delight, at rest—like Clarissa herself." (56) Clocks relate objects and people, their thoughts and actions, into a whole relationship.

Septimus could not communicate his innermost feelings and sentiments to mankind. It was only in time that he could perceive reality and therefore his act of self-annihilation and his transcendence to eternity. Virginia Woolf's schematization of both inner duration and external time is laudable. She proves her mastery over the time-technique in the novels which come after *Jacob's Room*. Clarissa and Septimus communicate subconsciously by clock-time. Conscious time merges past, present and future for the protagonists. Clarissa's internal monologue in the beginning of the novel takes us thirty years back, as does her meeting with Peter Walsh. Infinite time is ours, even though present time is governed by clocks—the leaden circles of Big Ben dissolving in the air.

Space is treated with a better perspective in *Mrs. Dalloway* than in Joyce's *Ulysses*. London is the arena, the scene of action, which is explored all round by the characters. Each character is spatialized in his area of business. They are united by the common sights they behold and are thus united temporally and spatially, like the sky-writing of the aeroplane. Virginia Woolf delineates it as a "concentration, a symbol . . . of man's soul."[18]

Space and time are two dimensions influencing literary style directly. Poulet is of the opinion that spatial distance is necessary from the conscious world:

> It is the prime task of man. It no longer consists in feeling, nor in striving to transform his sensation into sympathy or thought. A purely sensible being . . . can go only from sensation to sensation by an uninterrupted movement as harassing as it is vain. On the contrary, what man must do is break the sensuous enchantment and enchainment, turn aside from the actual, establish between what he has felt and what he is going to think, an intense distance, a zone of calm, of reserve, and of silence, in which the seed of thought will find the ground and the time necessary, over a long period in which to take shape.[19]

It is only through symbols that one can delve into abstractions of life. "What did it mean to her, this thing called life?" (40) Clarissa asks herself in *Mrs. Dalloway*. Social symbols are many, characterized by various personalities, like the Prime Minister, Lady Bruton, Whitbread, Sir William Bradshaw and Lady Bradshaw. These characterize the snobs, belonging to the higher strata of society who are the social symbols of aristocracy. London is a powerful and rich symbol of human alienation. When Virginia Woolf had a bout of insanity in 1921, she had to avoid excessive socialization and was sent to Richmond. This reminds us of Rachel Vinrace's lonely sojourn at Richmond. It is only later that Virginia Woolf was fascinated by the London streets and her solitary escapades fortified her privacy, amidst the vast sea of human beings, pervading her with ontological security. London is to Virginia Woolf what Dublin is to Joyce. The waves and sea imagery can be personified in the streets, together with a feeling of loneliness even in this deluge of human beings.

Virginia Woolf's party metaphor is not pleasantly portrayed. Individuality is utterly destroyed by excessive socialization. A party symbolizes groupism and demands socialistic traits. Clarissa thus is weighed down by her duties as a hostess. Socialization is juxtaposed with the kind of imagery wherein an individual can soar in the sky with absolute freedom. Scrope Purvis sees Clarissa with "a touch of the bird about her of the joy, blue-green, light vivacious," (6) Clarissa reminisces the "rocks, rising and falling," (5) and Septimus tries to reach out of the "Swallows swooping, swerving, flinging themselves, in and out." (77) A sparrow chirruped Septimus's name and another sparrow sang in Greek "from the meadows of life, beyond a river where there is no dead." (28) An individual finds peace and repose in the precincts of her own room. As John Graham says:

> In many of Mrs. Woolf's novels . . . the room symbolises the selfhood formed in time. From her small room, then, Clarissa looks out and sees the supreme mystery: that people exist in the same stream of time, each moving under the compulsion of the time-flow (as symbolised by Big Ben) visible to each other, yet unknown to each other and essentially alone.[20]

The closed car on Bond Street was a symbol of alienation, indicating an enclosed individual: "the agglomeration of mind around the motor car is paralleled by a physical drawing together of the cars, of persons and bicycles, in a visible manifestation of psychical occurrence . . . the motor car therefore is something more than a focus for attention, for extra-corporeal consciousness."[21]

Like the globe, the window symbolizes a great deal of truth in the novels of Virginia Woolf. Katharine Hilbery perceives Ralph Denham standing cold and forlorn outside her window and she instantly realizes her love for him. Rachel Vinrace used to look at the lights in Terence's window and evince his moods. In *Mrs. Dalloway,* the window has been elevated to a higher strata, symbolizing the outlook of an individual. Septimus asserts his individuality by jumping from a window, amidst a mass of humanity, defying time, space and the entire universe.

Peter Walsh's pocket-knife is a masculine symbol, denoting his patriarchal nature and will to dominate. It also signifies a source of self-confidence, along with his sense of identity and a form of self-defence. Coins play an important role to ascertain one's independence for essential freedom of an individual which was focussed in *A Room of One's Own* and *Jacob's Room.* In *Mrs. Dalloway*, it signified the union of two minds. The protagonist threw a shilling in the Serpentine in a delightful mood. Septimus's death occurs in a similar vein—jumping out of the window, never to return. She recalls: "She had once thrown a shilling into the Serpentine, never anything more. But he had flung it away." (203)

Animal imagery is a continuous process in Virginia Woolf's novels. Septimus Smith's fragile mental condition makes him desire solitude. His inability to communicate makes him appear disagreeable and abnormal. He feels disgusted: "For the truth is . . . that human beings have neither kindness, nor faith, ncr chastity beyond what serves to increase the pleasure of the moment, they hunt in packs. Their packs scour the desert, and vanish screaming into the wilderness" (135) and "repulsive brute, with blood-red nostrils." (139) At one stage, he even envisions an animal transformed to a man. (102)) The diamond imagery represents the glitter of a sul erficial society. Clarissa adorned in her glittering attire, moved among her equally glamorous guests enacting a role imposed by a lifestyle bearing her husband's name.

Shakespearean allusions figure strongly but are not a central feature as in *Night and Day*. Clarissa's expression, "Fear no more the heat of the sun,"[22] is cathartic by nature, an auto-suggestion to face life and society with renewed courage; her soul represented by Septimus Smith having paid with his life to social demands. Clarissa could now whole-heartedly accede to her superficial duties. When she reminisces her love for Sally in her youth: "If it were now to die; 'T were now to be most happy."[23] Septimus too quoted from Shakespeare's *Anthony and Cleopatra,* "the intoxication of language" and this inspiration, his artistic sensibility is projected in his dying moment: "He was not afraid. At every moment Nature signified . . . standing close up to breathe through her hallowed hands Shakespeare's words, her meaning." (154)

The novel commences with a glimpse into Clarissa's consciousness. Even though she was middle-aged, "she felt unspeakably young" and "at the same time unspeakably aged. She sliced like a knife through everything; at the same time was outside, looking on." (10)

Clarissa can be visualized walking on a London street on a lovely day in June but harbouring a whole lot of complexities in her subconscious. We also get acquainted with Peter Walsh, her former suitor, who had been away to India and her friend Sally Seton. She was infused in mankind but we can perceive only a fraction of her personality. Her inner being is of course longing to preserve her own identity. She therefore envies the old woman opposite her house: "But love and religion would destroy that whatever it was, the privacy of the soul." (139) Unfortunately her social existence denies her this luxury of her individuality. She is surrounded by her satellites and the narration is unified by the adroit juxtaposition of her past and present. Her soliloquies give us a glimpse of her inner being. Socially, she holds a supremely regal position but in reality, she is a warm and affectionate person, even though she tries to maintain a snobbish attitude in her social relationships. Virginia Woolf herself was a very lonely and forlorn individual. Her physical problems had deprived her of the pleasure of motherhood and a normal marital life. Thus in the role of Clarissa, she pervades this narration with her self-dejection:

> What did it mean to her, this thing called life? Oh, it was very queer. Here was so and so in South Kensington; some one up in Bays Water; and somebody else, say, in Mayfair. And she felt quiet continuously a sense of their existence; and she felt what a waste; and she felt what a pity; and she felt if only they

> could be brought together; so she did it. And it was an offering; to combine, to create; but to whom? (135)

Clarissa does enjoy social life but simultaneously she is obsessed with a sense of loneliness and isolation and a recurring terror of death. Her hectic social life robs her of something infinitely precious from her inner being and she is constantly oppressed by a sense of insecurity. She feels a sense of isolation and alienation as she detests the oppression of the group and crowd as seen in any type of social life. Her individual consciousness swings like a pendulum between the two types of consciousness—the alienated individual-consciousness and the suffocating group-consciousness. Thus at times, Clarissa has the feeling of being impoverished in her consciousness as she feels her incapacity of providing herself with the right type of sustenance. This feeling is unravelled in the unconscious working of her mind which is delineated in her disjointed thoughts—the stream of her consciousness. She is the pivot of the narrative and her individual consciousness evolves completely when focussing on the individuals around her. She is the titular heroine and her vigorous sense of individuality helps her to survive and her success is crowned by the title of the novel:

> she felt herself every where; not here, here, here, and she tapped the back of the seat; but every where. She waved her hand going up Shaftesbury Avenue. She was all that. So that to know her, or anyone, one must seek out the people who completed them; even the places. . . . It ended in a transcendental theory, which, with her horror of death, allowed her to believe, or say that she believed (for all her scepticism), that since our apparitions, the part of us, which spreads wide, the unseen might survive, be recovered somehow attached to this person or that, or even haunting certain places, after death. Perhaps—perhaps. (204)

In her interior monologues we are aware of Clarissa's personality and also that of another individual who will complete her individuality, namely the unseen part of her being. He is Septimus Warren Smith who was bordering on a condition of insanity as diagnosed by the doctors and society. By this subconscious relationship, Clarissa achieves a sense of identity and finally Septimus's death redeems the hollowness, the corruption and the lies and the useless chatter of her life.

Clarissa's relationship with her husband Richard was beautiful, all-pervasive, with no bindings on the surface but at heart, she could not transcend her inner barriers, desiring solitude:

> Like a nun withdrawing, or a child exploring a tower. . . . There was an emptiness about the heart of life. . . . Narrower and narrower would her bed be . . . she could not dispel a virginity preserved through childbirth which clung to her like a sheet. . . . She could see what she lacked; it was not beauty; it was not mind. It was something central which permeated; something warm which broke up surfaces and rippled the cold contact of man and woman, or of women together. (34-36)

Freud has discovered that homosexual traits are present in every case of neurosis. In the case of Virginia Woolf, her homosexual tendency can be analyzed from two angles. On the demise of her mother, when she was only thirteen, she was sexually abused by her two step-brothers George and Gerald Duckworth. These distasteful experiences caused permanent damage to her natural sexual instincts for the opposite sex. Maybe we can trace this as another singular cause for her neurotic disposition, having to silently forbear the sexual onslaughts of the two brutal men. She had lost her mother, the only woman to whom she could run for shelter, and this protection was banished from her forever.

This innate desire for a mother's touch, combined with her bitter physical experience with men, evolved an attraction for intimate relationship with women. Freud's theory is partly applicable to Virginia Woolf's homosexual tendency because we cannot dispute the fact that she was a neurotic; unfortunately the root cause of her neurosis would not interest society and that is the irony of life.

A woman's helplessness can embitter her very existence but society misinterprets her sorrow. Inner disunion in a child is the prototype of an important psychological phenomena—the splitting of consciousness which will be visible in various forms in adult life:

> The starting point for the feminine tendencies of the neurotic is the child's feeling of weakness in the face of adults. From this arises a need for support, a demand for affection, a physiological and psychological dependence and submission, In cases of early and subjectively felt organ inferiority these traits are intensified. Increased dependency and the intensified feeling of our own littleness and weakness lead to inhibition of aggression and thereby to the phenomenon of anxiety.[24]

It is these negative psychic processes which structure mental ailments like neurasthenia, hysteria and paranoia. These denote the maladjustment of the inner masculine and feminine forces inherent in all individuals, erupting in a series of neurotic protests. Psychotherapy is the medical solution to unravel these complicated dynamics and bring the patient to normalcy. Virginia Woolf's ideas were channelled in other directions. She detested psychiatrists and preferred to upgrade the mental health of suffering people by bringing about radical changes in our social set-up, by transforming certain traditional customs which caused more destruction than good. Subjection of women was the burning topic of her thoughts and the vindication of one's individuality in tradition-bound society.

In Septimus Smith and Jacob Flanders, Woolf has projected men who failed to adjust amidst unnerving social forces. According to Adler, neurosis is a defense of the ego; this may cohere to Virginia Woolf's feminist ideas, to her subjugated childhood, sublimation of facilities in order to cater to her brother's education and the sexual molestations. Since vociferous protests were impossible, the suppression of extreme emotions resulted in neurasthenia. These deplorable state of affairs caused infinite damage to the psychic mechanisms in individuals causing sensitive minds to react considerably. According to her, social changes in the right direction should displace psychoanalysis or mental therapy.

Our mental life is governed by various forces and voluntary and involuntary impulses which constitute our personality. We should attempt to orient our inner lives towards healthy goals and overcome psychological impediments prevalent in our inner and outer worlds. We can evince Clarissa's homosexual tendency in the final words of the passage quoted above. In her youth at Bourton, she was in love with Sally Seton, a youthful, fun-loving girl: "then came the most exquisite moment of her whole life—passing a stone urn with flowers in it. Sally stopped; picked a flower, kissed her on the lips. The whole world might have turned upside down. The others disappeared; here she was alone with Sally." (40) The incident has a biographical element, Sally and her personality. Unfortunately, Virginia Woolf's life was threatened with insanity which was inherited from her cousin and step-sister. She was a witness to their insane manners. Having a very sensitive disposition which had a lasting impression on her, she faced her first mental breakdown at the tender age of thirteen. Her step-brother's sexual overtures precipitated matters. Dr. Seton was their family physician and she dearly loved him. She christened Sally with his name. But Sally Seton was the embodiment of her friend Madge Symonds who was a romantic figure residing in the Alps and a writer with a melancholic strain pervading her being, whom Virginia Woolf was truly in love with.

Peter Walsh had indirectly disrupted this relationship when they fell in love with each other. At present he is fifty-three years old, jobless, in love with a widow and in his subconscious still in love with Clarissa. The old woman's song outside Regent's Park places him as a solitary traveller in this universe. Peter's sudden arrival assuaged her depression, giving momentary sustenance to the impoverished soul. But his was an unstable personality, frustrated and dependent, with contradictory qualities leading to isolation. As Leaska writes: "Such are the peculiar constituents of a man with a brittle emotional architecture held together by rivets of anger and fear."[25] This is the vision of a man for whom "Nothing exists outside us except a state of mind . . . a desire for solace, for relief, these feeble, these ugly, these craven men and women." (85) His pocket-knife is his protection, a psychological defence in case of attack. Septimus and Walsh are on a similar plane of instability and complex existence. They feel like outcasts in society and cannot adjust to its infinite demands. Like Septimus and Clarissa, Walsh prefers solitude and wonders whether he should attend her party. His thoughts delve into the philosophy of life:

> For this is the truth about our soul, he thought, our self, who fish-like inhabits deep seas and plies among obscurities threading her way between the pools of giant weeds, over sun-flickered spaces on and on into gloom, cold, deep, inscrutables suddenly she shoots to the surface and sports on the wind-wrinkled waves; that is, has a positive need to brush, scrape, kindle herself, gossiping. (178)

The one similarity between Peter and Doris Kilman was that they were not enamoured by Clarissa's social life—"her delicate body, her air of freshness and fashion." (138) Clarissa did not harbour any love for Miss Kilman either: "Agh, how she hated her—hot, hypocritical, corrupt; with all that power, Elizabeth's seducer; the woman who had crept in to steal and defile. . . . She hated her; she loved her. It was enemies one wanted, not friends." (265) Miss Kilman teaches Modern History to Elizabeth, "the female counterpart of Sir William Bradshaw; her existence overshadows the life of Clarissa as Sir William does that of Septimus."[26] She is an emancipated woman, religious and self-righteous, distorting her sensibility. She had starved herself for the cause of the Austrians. Now, even in her emancipation, she got no life; she talked aloud at times: "It is the flesh, it is the flesh." (142)

Clarissa envisioned her as a tyrant and vampire but Miss Kilman herself was the victim of patriarchy who had robbed her of education and reduced her to poverty. Now, the Church was the only source of reassurance and it had alleviated her suffering. Her desire to possess Elizabeth is replaced by her gorging of food; a complex-ridden, frustrated woman, having no joy in living. Septimus and Kilman shared a disgust and hatred for mankind.

Septimus's sense of reality could only be understood and comprehended by him alone and the world considered him insane because of this. He never could identify himself with society. Isolation was the only method by which he could find a meaning in life. His vision of universal brotherhood and his hatred for crime was very apparent in his thought-processes. His body was macerated until only the nerve fibres were left. It was spread like a veil upon the rock. (142) Lucrezia desperately tries to involve him with the outside world so as to enable him to communicate his emotions but Septimus in a desperate attempt to preserve his security ends his life. Lucrezia tries to rationalize his perception of life but in the process destroys his individuality. Silence and solitude are compulsory factors in the preservation of an individual's sanity in this complex society. Thus Jacob Flanders, Rachel Vinrace and Katharine Hilbery flee from group-activities either to the sanctity of nature or to the security of their rooms. These sensitive souls turn to nature for solace because it nourishes these spiritual and aesthetic selves, helping them to retain their individual consciousness.

In T.S. Eliot's poem, *The Love Song of Alfred J. Prufrock*, the protagonist possesses a highly sensitive and artistic consciousness and, like Septimus, wonders at the outside world. His extreme sensitivity makes activity impossible and he is in danger of losing his fine sensibility. This inner agony of the consciousness of the protean self of an individual, remarks Grillet, is heightened in modern psychological novels.[27]

Virginia Woolf's artistic frame of mind could not tolerate any form of torture and pain caused to an individual. She was so terrified of the cruelty and death brought about by the war that her disgust was shown in the fear complex that had developed as a result of Septimus's experiences in the war.

Evan's death was the undoing of Septimus and his only defence against life was death. Similarly, in William Faulkner's *The Sound and the Fury*, Benjy's life is based on the unconscious level of experience outside the region of temporal order as all unconscious processes are timeless. But his memory is sharp and he recalls the past realistically, as did Septimus, when he sees Evans walking up to him, absolutely healthy, with no ravages of the war visible on him. Nobody could reach out to his true being, his real self, imbued in the aesthetics of life, neither can he respond to this hypocritical, superficial, social existence, but drew peace and solace from nature. Looking up at the aeroplane, his response was in the affirmative:

> So, thought Septimus, looking up, they are signalling to me. Not indeed in actual words: that is, he could not read the language yet; but it was plain enough, this beauty, this exquisite beauty, and tears filled his eyes as he looked up at the smoke, words languishing and melting in the sky and bestowing upon him, in their inexhaustible charity and laughing goodness, one shape after another of unimaginable beauty and signalling their intention to provide him, for nothing, for ever, for looking merely, with beauty, more beauty. Tears ran down his cheeks. (25)

What a pathetic rendition of a trapped soul, vainly attempting to grasp a fraction of the beauteous nature, absorb it, feel it, and tears run down at its exquisite beauty! Virginia Woolf has portrayed her own struggle to break all barriers of the outside world and cross these abysses of darkness and reach a world wherein she can exist peacefully with her individuality intact. Her personal experience was utilized in the characterization of Septimus at a deeper level than our superficial existence:

> I adumbrate here a study of insanity and suicide, the worlds seen by the sane and insane side by side.[28]
>
> Of course the mad part tries me so much, makes my mind squirt so badly that I can hardly face spending the next weeks as it is.[29]

As we read the development of Septimus's insanity, we can visualize Virginia Woolf experiencing similar agony, as recorded by her husband Leonard Woolf in his autobiography, "the doctors called it neurasthenia . . . a name which covered a multitude of sins, symptoms, and miseries of manic depressive insanity."[30]

Psychological tolerance is squarely based on social relations. If the individual is confronted with problems beyond his acceptance, then we find a change from normal behaviour, which is a deviation towards neurosis. Insecurity in childhood resulting from domination either by societal norms or family members is projected: "Compensation of psychological effort which often strikes out along new and different paths in order to deal with the tensions of life and so cover up a felt deficiency."[31]

Marriage was no solution, leaving them lonelier than ever. Psychiatric help proved to be even more hazardous. Dr. Holmes proved to be a crude, hardened man with no knowledge of gentle and delicate approach to his patients because he was morally responsible for their well-being. These doctors psychologically devoured their patients, leaving no trace of their minds. Sir Bradshaw is an eminent psychologist with a 'home' where he forces individuals to set their perspectives of life as per social demands. His sense of proportion and conversion discards humanistic values, brutally exposing the problems of his patients, pushing them into even more dire straits of insecurity. Septimus proferred to accept his riot-ridden being and sacrifice his soul, in order to retrieve his individuality and preserve a unified whole of his being. Virginia Woolf was deeply suspicious of psychiatrists who can uproot an individual's existence from the face of this earth. She was denied motherhood because they had convinced her husband that motherhood would affect her health negatively:

> Worshipping proportion, Sir William not only prospered himself but made England prosper, secluded her lunatics, forbade childbirth, penalised despair, made it impossible for the unfit to propagate their views until they too shared his sense of proportion—his, if they were men, Lady Bradshaw's

if they were women. (110)

Characters who failed to adjust in society were literally crucified by the author since such a life to her was a living death. We can have a few characters like those of Jacob, Mrs. Ramsay, Rachel Vinrace, Mary Datchet and Septimus Smith. Religion is not conspicuously present but is diffused in a veiled manner because it is inherent in every individual and the gulf between art and religion cannot be made too wide.

The structure of *Mrs. Dalloway* is on two levels of consciousness signified by two individuals—Clarissa Dalloway and Septimus Warren Smith. Septimus is a symbol of her inner consciousness. At one point Clarissa is a social recluse, unable to intermingle in society. At another juncture, she is in the centre of social life. She is therefore precariously balanced between her individual consciousness and her positive response to her party-consciousness where she suffers mental and physical alienation: "But often now this body she wore . . . this body with all its capacities, seemed nothing—nothing at all." (13) Her individuality was smothered by the glamour and glitter of society, putting her at variance with her instincts. A similar situation is reflected in R.D. Laing's book *Divided Self* which describes a schizophrenic patient who maintained himself in isolated detachment from the world for months, living alone in a single room where he began to feel he was dying inside. As his state of depersonalization progressed he would emerge into social life for a brief foray in order to get a "dose of other people, but not an overdose."[32] Mrs. Dalloway has a strong personality by which she can integrate her individual vision with the group-consciousness; Septimus, on the other hand, failed to do so and was left unprotected from the onslaughts of society, including the murderous psychiatrists. His wife Lucrezia too found it difficult to adjust with him as he was apparently a paranoid and insane man but was actually an individual who responded to life with an intensity which normal people could not accept.

An individual endowed with a refined sensibility will inherently possess the trait of solipsism. Such men have narcissist leanings because of their involvement with the self. They seek reality which they can never find in the material aspects but only in truth, not in society but in a single epiphanous moment. Like Peter Walsh who in a moment of epiphany realized that Clarissa would definitely marry Richard Dalloway and though he was drowned in sorrow, that was a moment of truth which he had to face.

Death played an important role in Virginia Woolf's life. At the tender age of thirteen she lost her mother, causing her first mental breakdown. Later she lost her step-sister Stella, her father and brother Thoby:

> Once more my mind is distracted from the thought of death. I am suspended between life and death in an unfamiliar way.[33]

Violet Dickinson took her home to Burnham Wood. It was here that she attempted to commit suicide by throwing herself down from a window. It is in this aspect that we can draw a similarity with Septimus who was Clarissa's subconscious self:

> "One must write down deep feelings," said Dostoevsky. And do I? Or do I fabricate with words loving them as I do? No I think not. In this book I have almost too many ideas. I want to give life and death, sanity and insanity. I want to criticise the social system and show it to work at its most intense.[34]

In *Mrs. Dalloway*, the dignified hostess is not the real Clarissa. All her husband's glittering offerings cannot negate the feeling of insufficiency within her. Septimus personifies this sensitive malaise-ridden, inner soul of Clarissa. His death is her triumph, a projection of the invisible portion of her being battling against the many forces of nature; a revolt against the demons of society personified by William Bradshaw and Holmes: "A feeling of depression is on me, being at low ebb with my book, the death of Septimus . . . and I begin to count myself as a failure." (165) But it is in Septimus's death that Clarissa communicates with him. Death does not for once annihilate but unites two beings in an intense moment of consciousness. Septimus jumps from the window, saying, "I will give it to you," (203) indirectly expressing Clarissa's lifestyle of giving joy to others being her very existence. She is relieved to hear of his death, remembering the shilling she had thrown in the Serpentine: "But he had flung it away," (165) not a shilling but his very life:

> A thing there was that mattered, a thing, wreathed about with chatter, defaced, obscured in her own life, let drop every day in corruption, lies, chatter. This he had preserved. Death was defiance. Death was an attempt to communicate, people feeling the impossibility of reaching the centre which mystically, evaded them, closeness drew apart, rapture faded, one was alone. There was an embrace in death. (204)

For Clarissa, life and death were the two forms of extreme involvement. Sex, the intermediary force, the desire inherent in most individuals, was destroyed in her youth by her cousin George Duckworth: "The sheets were clean, tight-stretched in a broad white band from side to side. Narrower and narrower would her bed be." (35) She repudiated sex, the life force, earlier predicted by Peter as the "death of the soul" at Bourton. She walked out of the room when Sally had made an open remark regarding a neighbour's adulterous behaviour. But there was an innate need in her for platonic relationships. Peter was the only character in the novel who could gauge her as an individual with her complexes and desires. They would have been perfectly matched but for Clarissa's fear of being dominated by Peter. She did not experience any real pleasure in their marital life because he could not perceive her from the angle which really mattered. Her spirit was only hers, and he could not share that mysticism with her. The only positive factor was that her life was her own and she flourished in solitude. Even amidst a party, she could identify with her own self which is the subtlety of Virginia's technique. Malcolm Lowry's *Under the Volcano* and Hemingway's *Old Man and the Sea* have attenuated this technique. Geoffery's alcoholic hallucinations are interrupted by external reality—irrelevant conversations, words from a travel-folder, posters in the street. Yvonne's flow of experience confuses memory, desire and the present moment. Such mental complexities are as customary as the use of symbols for deeper meaning. *Under the Volcano,* like *Mrs. Dalloway*, is a narration of one day in 1938 in Mexico City. The surface "hides a deeper significance of which the characters and their actions are symbolic."

Tindall is of the opinion that Joyce's *Ulysses* is the flowering of Stephen's genius. Since Mrs. Bloom is the heart of the book, she is not only the flower of vision but the fruit that Mrs. Bloom offers the still-frustrated poet in a dream. Her fruitiness accepted by Stephen is established by Bloom's final act of the day.[36] This incidence filters into our consciousness by the three protagonists. This trinity of characters resembles Clarissa, Richard and Peter where Peter penetrates the depth of Clarissa's soul and Richard and Clarissa are only on a superficial level, with Elizabeth as the insignia of the relationship. Alan Kennedy in his book *The Protean Self* has mentioned Cicourel's Cognitive Society: "Individual behaviour according to their established roles in society, a cognitive centre wherein the individual is briefed about his actions, giving rise to 'surface structures' from the base of the 'deep structures,' which are inherent parts of the protean self."

The defenceless individual, reticent by nature is seen in the character of Septimus Smith, a victim of our ruthless society and the indifferent manner in which the death of his friend Evan was received by his acquaintances. For Clarissa, the announcement of Septimus's death pervades the atmosphere magically with serenity and harmony. Clarissa experiences a feeling of holy communion, she felt as though her own being had experienced it. She felt purified and purged of all the dissatisfaction and uneasiness which had prevailed upon her. Peter too overcomes temporal and spatial barriers and unites with her on a similar plane of consciousness. He had misjudged her all these years and had failed to penetrate the physical barriers to the beautiful being within. Septimus constantly clashed with society and she glided along amidst people as if with her sails unfurled, sailing with the mood prevalent. Her desire to live affirms her life socially but Septimus preferred death because living amidst sordid materialism and untruth would have been an act of sacrifice by his soul. Clarissa does not fear death but faces life boldly. A certain unfulfilled portion of Clarissa's being, a certain unexposed need is fulfilled with Septimus's death. She rejuvenates herself and begins anew, drenched in a new-found joy and individuality. It was her enlightenment in the ante-room, watching the old woman and acknowledging her relationship with Septimus. The unfulfilled being was suddenly overflowing with a sense of completion, there was the realization of an unexpressed and inviolable streak suppressed all these years and beautifully illuminated in this moment of epiphany. This party triggers off many relationships—the reunion of Clarissa and Peter, her renewed lease of existence and Peter's moment of epiphany too, in accepting Clarissa's social role, "For there she was." (213)

Avrom Fleishman comments on the relationship of Clarissa and Septimus from the mythical point of view:

> In recent studies of myth and archetype, such movements of the hero are called patterns of "withdrawal and return"—a temporary removal from the active role, a pause for meditation and inspiration, and a rededication to the social group and its destiny . . . we may say, then, there is a division of function within the conjoining protagonist of *Mrs. Dalloway;* while Septimus plays the role of a sacrificial object—scapegoat or dying god. Clarissa plays the role of the social leader who temporarily withdraws for insight into the true significance of a leader's role and for rededication to it; Septimus as the outcaste whose death reinvigorates his society and is matched by Clarissa as a social organiser who raises her activity from mindless social climbing to a principled life of affirmation.[38]

In reality, Virginia Woolf acquiesced to the worldly society, presumed her own mental disability and, like Septimus Smith, blew out the candle of her life by drowning in a river. These are the pages wherein she bared her heart and soul: "I think it is the most satisfactory of my novels . . . it seems to leave me plunged deep in the richest strata of my mind"[39]:

> I should say a good deal about *The Hours (Mrs. Dalloway)* and my discovery, how I dig I think that gives exactly what I want, humanity, humour, depth. The idea is that the caves shall connect, and each comes to daylight at the present moment.[40]

Virginia Woolf's poetic style and urge for solitude are visible in all her literary creations. She was enamoured by the very word sublime which reflected her trend of thought:

> Pseudo-Longinus saw the sublime as a powerful natural force reflecting the greatness of God who had a profound philosophical meaning and could help solve the problem of the meaning of life.[41]

She comprehended the mundane amidst an aura of sublime beauty moulded in a lyrical language.

The two major social cataclysms that Virginia Woolf abhorred was the subjugated status of women in society and the complete dominance of an individual by society wherein absolute individuation resulted in either being called insane or to find permanent peace in taking one's own life.

Tragedy pervades life or society, but never in its entirety. A complete personality can be achieved only by determining perfect social interaction. An individual should initially develop his inner being which will form the structural base and then relate with the outside world on a perfect footing.

Yuri Borev in his book *Aesthetics: The Sociology of Art* points out that "Auto Communication" can be carried out in two ways. The first is a silent inner monologue; the second, through the relations between the conscious and subconscious mind. The method has been discovered by realistic art which has mastered the method of psychological analysis and was able to describe the stream-of-consciousness in its relation to society and the subconscious processes, in their connection with consciousness and in their manifestation through speech.[42]

Projecting life in reality proves the depth and quality of the artist's consciousness and Virginia Woolf justifies this concept perfectly. Her "tunnelling process" projects the past as a mirror:

> 19th century realism has shown that man's consciousness shaped in the process of his psyche embraces all his life experience. . . . This is not just communication with the world but mutual enrichment. The consciousness reflects and transforms the world, while the world shapes the consciousness. Henri Pieron, the French psychologist, called a new-born baby "a candidate for the position of man" who attains the status of a full-fledged member of the human race only after a certain minimum of social and historical experience has become his. In this, he is assisted by mental activity.[43]

The following few lines composed by John Donne integrate man and society on a plane indicating the highest level of consciousness, in perfect communion and harmony "any man's death diminishes me, because I am involved in Mankind; And therefore never send to know for whom the bell tolls; It tolls for thee."

III

If *Mrs. Dalloway* was projection of Virginia Woolf's personality, *To the Lighthouse* is a very sensitive portrayal of Virginia Woolf's years of childhood spent at St. Ives where the Godrevy lighthouse was situated. The Lighthouse is the central symbol of the novel. The indecision, insanity, excessive socialization of Mrs. Dalloway is here distilled to a peaceful and serene existence exhibiting a greater degree of maturity depicted by the stoic powerful symbol of the lighthouse. Mrs. Ramsay is undaunted by the constant flux of people and her complete involvement with her family. Nothing obtrudes on to the inner sphere of her individuality. She becomes one with its beams and this mystical experience transcends her to realms unknown. It is an inextricable limb of the ocean as Mrs. Ramsay is of her home. Though this is a syncretic vision, it cannot be nullified, being a realistic part of life—a union of self and reality. David Daiches comments:

> The Lighthouse . . . standing lonely in the midst of the sea, is a symbol of the individual who is at once a unique being and a part of the flux of history. To reach the Lighthouse is, in a sense, to make contact with truth outside oneself, to surrender the uniqueness of one's ego to an impersonal reality.[44]

Herbert Marder points out that the tower is masculine and the sea feminine, a radiance joining these two aspects, a symbol of the marriage of opposites, implying the androgynous mind.[45]

The technique Virginia Woolf utilizes in this novel makes a complete break from the nineteenth-century tradition, projecting the inner reality minus the chaotic and incoherent style of *Jacob's Room* and *Mrs. Dalloway*. This novel is given a more organized outlook and the narration presents a beautifully textured fabric, interwoven with the author's leitmotifs of time and consciousness. It projects a multidimensional picture by the juxtapositioning of interior monologues as in Joyce's *Ulysses* where the consciousness of Stephen, Molly and Leopold Bloom are in opposition to each other. The transfusion of the various consciousnesses interlaced by time is visualized by Mitchell Leaska:

> What we want to know, however, is how past events or the expectations of the future have been or will be assimilated by the individual consciousness; we want to know how each mind feels about what has happened or what is happening or what might happen. Through a progression of interior views, this continual ebb and flow of interior illumination, our interest is aroused to the degree that we want to continue reading until the whole tapestry of experience is revealed and felt.[46]

The unconscious plays a vital role in this technique of narration. We delve into our subconscious if we have the capacity to come out with original creativity. D.H. Lawrence also gave importance to this aspect and has proliferated his thoughts in a book, *The Fantasia of the Unconscious and Psychoanalysis and the Unconscious* describing it as "the spontaneous life motive in every organism (for) it begins where life begins."[47] It is only by the direct descent into the consciousness of her characters that Virginia Woolf can penetrate into the labyrinthine alleys of life and delve into its basic truths and realities. Bernard Blackstone suggests subject-object diffusion when he says that Mrs. Woolf's characters have an aura of consciousness in which her readers participate.[48] Regarding the theme of this novel, the author recorded her thoughts in her diary:

> This is going to be fairly short, to have father's character done complete in it and mother's, and St. Ives; and childhood. . . . But the centre is father's character, sitting in a boat, reciting 'we perished, each alone,' while he crushes a dying mackerel.[49]

Forty-three years later, Virginia Woolf unravelled these memories from the knotted reeds of her mind.

The human psyche is a complex entity and it needs skilful handling, with the right association of ideas, symbols and language for the perfect presentation of this oceanic subject. *To the Lighthouse,* though a psychological novel, is demarcated into three parts and moulded perfectly in the required temporal schemata. Its three-part structure has "Window," "Time Passes" and "The Lighthouse," portraying a succession of changes in a span of ten years, with life and death interspersed dialectically in a mythopoetic style. Its loose structure could easily incorporate all spheres of life, be it social, religious, moral or individualistic. This caters to Roger Fry's aesthetic design for a perfect literary architecture. Presentation of sensitive moments in a suitable format enriches the narrative, the reader literally experiencing the sensations in a realistic manner. The structure is determined by a psychological dialectic. The central conflict is the hostility between James the youngest son and his father Mr. Ramsay, a basic question of the Oedipus Complex. Secondly, the emotional maladjustment of two major personalities Mr. and Mrs. Ramsay where she experiences the disparity to a greater degree but is able to comouflage it because she loves her husband. Finally, we see the author's struggle to project the artistic sensation in the personality of Lily Briscoe. Virginia Woolf's personal dilemma regarding the form of the novel can be deciphered from this passage:

> The first fruit of the CR (*Common Reader*, 1925) [a book too highly praised now] is a request to write for the Atlantic Monthly. So I am getting pushed into criticism. It is a great standby—this power to make large sums by formulating views on Stendhal and Swift. But while I try to write, I am making up *To the Lighthouse*--sea is to be heard all through it. I have an idea that I will invent a new name for my books to supplant 'novel.' A new— by Virginia Woolf. But what? Elegy?[50]

The multiple viewpoint method is Woolf's chosen technique to narrate her story. The scene of the dinner party gives a kaleidoscopic view of eight individuals with varied personalities, juxtaposed in a particular spatial angle, and their conversation interwoven temporally—by the past, present and future. The omniscient narrator projects her own personal viewpoints from various angles. The following gives us an idea of her narrative technique—verbal talk, interspersed with the working of the consciousness and authorial intervention and appropriate grammatical shifts:

> "It is a triumph," said Mr. Bankes, laying his knife down for a moment. He had eaten attentively. It was rich; it was tender. It was perfectly cooked. How did she manage these things in the depth of the country? he asked her. She was a wonderful woman. All his love, all his revernence had returned; and she

> knew it.
>
> "It is a French recipe of my grandmother's," said Mrs. Ramsay . . . till Lily thought, How childlike, how absurd she was, sitting up there with all her beauty opened again in her, talking about the skins of vegetables.[31]

The greatness of Virginia Woolf's novel lies in her weaving a variously patterned and beautiful fabric within a limited span of time. The motifs are sprinklings of impression by the skilful juxtaposition of the characters and their thought-processes within a prescribed temporal sphere—parenthetically disclosing the death of three individuals and the success of a person in the literary world. She deals with human relationship with masterly confidence but it is an enigma to most people. She deciphered the intricacies of this vital aspect of our existence, consciousness being the main instrument for communication and only a sensitive visionary like her could portray it convincingly. We can evince a clear picture of the inner lives of her characters—like Mrs. Ramsay—the semi-transparent envelop surrounding her and giving her an air of ethereality:

> Was it wisdom? Was it knowledge? Was it, once more, the deceptiveness of beauty, so that all one's perceptions, half-way to truth, were tangled in a golden mesh? or did she lock up within her some secret which certainly Lily Briscoe believed people must have for the world to go on at all? . . . Sitting on the floor with her arms round Mrs. Ramsay's knees, close as she could get, smiling to think that Mrs. Ramsay would never know the reason of that pressure, she imagined how in the chambers of the mind and heart of the woman who was, physically, touching her, where stood, like the treasures in the tombs of kings, tablets bearing sacred inscriptions, which if one could spell them out would teach one everything . . . which one pressed through into those secret chambers? What device for becoming, like waters poured into one jar, inextricably the same, one with the object one adored? Could the body achieve it, or the mind, subtly mingling in the

intricate passages of the brain? or the heart? (77)

Here we get a glimpse into Virginia Woolf's technique, her delving into the dark abyss of an individual's being, bringing into the open his inner thoughts and feelings.

Virginia Woolf's concept of art and her philosophy of life are beautifully amalgamated in this classical sensationalist formula: "There is nothing in the intellect that was not previously in the senses."[52]

Sensory experience is vital to creativity and Virginia Woolf was opposed to the excessive importance which was bestowed on rational thinking and intellect. This was acknowledged drastically in the philosophy of Lenin: "The first premise of the theory of knowledge undoubtedly is that the sole source of our knowledge is sensation."[53] Virginia Woolf's novels are sensitive creations and most of her women protagonists, though tremulous and vulnerable, delicately portray the various nuances of their minds.

This novel is Woolf's supreme experiment of internal impressionism, her most visionary and poetic creation which can be called a lyrical novel. Mr. Ramsay is a Professor of Philosophy and is holidaying on an island in the Hebrides along with his wife, children and few friends. It is late September, just before the outbreak of the First World War. The guests are varied: Lily Briscoe is an artist, William Bankes a contractor, Tansley a student, Carmichael a retired gentleman, Paul and Minta the two youngsters. James Ramsay is the youngest son and, like his mother and Lily Briscoe, has a sensitive nature. He is extremely excited over the proposed visit to the Lighthouse which however does not materialize. His feelings towards his father are extremely unfriendly. After the holiday, they leave the island and then the war breaks out. Ten years pass and the house is now in a state of decay. Mrs. Ramsay dies, Prue dies in childbirth and Andrew Ramsay is killed in the war. The remaining family once again visit the island of Skye in the company of Lily and Carmichael. James and his sister Cam visit the lighthouse along with Mr. Ramsay. It is here that all their hatred vanishes and peace and harmony prevail. It is also at this very moment that

Lily completes her picture and realizes her quest for a vision of "reality" which she can transfuse in colours on to her canvas. Josephine O'Brien Schaefer writes:

> *Time Passes* is the necessary link between the two. The cosmic perspective which has persistently added its peculiar quality to Virginia Woolf's previous novels has now come to the fore. In contrast Part II performs an important technical function, giving the reader space in which to allow experience to change into memory by the alchemy of time. It wrenches the reader out of the human sphere and rinses the mind of its perpetual concern with flesh and blood before introducing the human being again in the centre of the stage.[54]

We can get a glimpse of the process of the evolution of this novel from the entry in the author's diary:

> Yesterday I finished the first part of *To the Lighthouse* and today began the second. I cannot make it out here is the most difficult abstract piece of writing—I have to give an empty house, no people's characters, the passage of time; all eyeless and featureless with nothing to cling to; well, I rush at it, and at once scatter out two pages. Is it nonsense, is it brilliance?[55]

Language is subject to the thought-process of the author. Lyricism is purely a subjective style, expressing a personal emotion. In this novel, "Time Passes" is the most lyrical chapter wherein the author diffuses the temporal and spatial aspects in a depersonalized manner, with the usage of "we" and "one." Her prose style is rampant with poetic rhythms, imagery and repetition.

The novel is succinctly divided in two spheres, that of prose and poetry, depicting the intellectual and rational individuals, demarcated by the intuitive and sensitive class of people, interwoven with the mysteries of life and death, the elemental experiences pervading the world. To transcribe these from sensations to reality was an inordinately delicate task for any author venturing out to project psychological realism in words.

The diffusion of time lends an aura of timelessness. In *Mrs. Dalloway*, it was a single-day sequence and in this novel it is a rendition of two days with a temporal gap of ten years. "Moments of Vision" form an intricate pattern in all her narratives. Bergson's theory of "inner-time" and "clock-time" comprises of only a few hours including a dinner party in the first chapter. But the psychological flow of time moves rapidly. A simple process of measuring a stocking reveals vistas of thoughts, fusing the past and present. As John Graham says, "Mrs. Ramsay has the power to see what Clarissa finally saw, the transfiguration of time by eternity."[56]

The processes of consciousness in "The Window" scene, include shifts of time and space in inner time. Erich Auerbach in *The Brown Stocking* stresses Virginia Woolf's multipersonal representation of consciousness, synthesizing the narrative temporally and spatially because an individual's thought-processes can traverse forward and backward freely, with no inhibitions. Marcel Proust's *A Le Recherche Du Temps Perdu* has a similar setting, delving into the past, moving back and forth, and retrieving diffused realities.

James Hafley quotes a passage of Tolstoy which includes time and space for true spiritual existence, which reflects in the character of Mrs. Ramsay:

> True life exists where the living being is conscious of itself as an indivisible "I," in whom all impressions, feelings etc. become one. So long as the "I" struggles, as nearly the whole animal world does, merely to crush other creatures known to him, in order to attain his own temporary advantage, true spiritual life which is without time and space remains unexpressed and imprisoned. True spiritual life is liberated when man neither rejoices in his own happiness, nor suffers from his own suffering, but suffers and rejoices with the worries and pleasures of others and is fused with them into a common life.[57]

We are surrounded by space in various forms and colours but spatial specificity is avoided, except for the holiday-camp at the Isle of Skye, somewhere in the Hebrides. Still and empty spatial presentation is given importance:

> The grey-green light on the wall opposite. The empty places. Such were some of the parts, but how bring them together? (220)
>
> And so lightly and swiftly pausing, striking, she scored her canvas with brown running nervous lines which had no sooner settled there than they enclosed (she felt it looming out at her) a space . . . what could be more formidable than that space? (179-80)

A fraction of empty space is personified with movement indicating life. The beam of the lighthouse illuminates a particular area of space, similar to Mrs. Ramsay's visionary being, spreading her beam of kindness and good cheer to all individuals in her sphere of life. Lily's art also revolves around space. Like Mrs. Ramsay and artists like Cezanne and Roger Fry, she aspired for "that still space that lies in the heart of things, where one could move or rest." (228) Quantitative space is the sacred space present in all human beings which can be transgressed by insensitive souls. Cassirer writes:

> Every position and direction in mythical space is endowed as it were with a particular accent and this accent always goes back to a fundamental mythical accent, the division between the sacred and the profane. . . . The primary spatial difference between two provinces of being, a common, generally accessible province and another, sacred, precinct which seems to be raised out of its surroundings hedged around and guarded against them.[58]

This invisible sphere is inspatial by nature because it does not occupy physical space but plays a dominant role in our being—the sacred space which all Woolf's visionary protagonists possess. Another symbol consistently mentioned in the first five of her novels is the lighthouse—a beacon of hope, inaccessible in normal circumstances and unaffected by natural elements.

The only path which is open to mankind to reveal realistically the vistas of hidden meaning in this universe and life's profundities is by the aid of appropriate images and symbols. Animal- and bird-imagery are an important form of characterization. Mr. Ramsay is delineated in bird-like imagery: "fierce as a hawk," (49) "like a desolate sea-bird," (68) "a famished" wolfhound, and "a wolf barking in the snow," (297) an elusive bird: "You might try to lay hands on him, but then like a bird, he spread his wings, he floated off to settle out of your reach somewhere far away on some desolate stump." (302)

Nature is an important image, depicting the passage of time. We can evince this from the ruined garden, the decline of order and serenity, necessarily ending in death and decay, "one feather, and the house, sinking, falling, would have turned and pitched downwards to the depths of darkness." (302) The ravaged autumn trees, symbolize Mr. Ramsay's lonely being after his wife's demise.

Throughout the book there is colour symbolism. Lily's struggle to depict reality through the medium of colour was initially unsuccessful as she struggled with the bright violet and vacant white. But when she did finally realize her vision, the lighthouse appeared to have unified with the blue haze of the atmosphere. Her impersonality was depicted with blue, Mr. Ramsay's rational being with red and brown.

The window is the most important symbol that Virginia Woolf utilizes in all her novels. Mrs. Ramsay and James are seated and Lily attempts to capture the scene with colour. Mrs. Ramsay insists on closed doors because they give her a feeling of security and open windows for freshness and to commune with nature.

The window also holds a sentimental place in the author's mind because a painting of her mother was framed against a window. If we read Woolf's books carefully, we will find a character standing at a window or looking through a window. It also conveys an individual transcending physical barriers and becoming one with the truth of nature.

Woolf's characters are variously portrayed. Katharine Hilbery was terrified of domesticity because it would inhibit her perusal of mathematics. Mrs. Dalloway was a combination of domesticity and society, co-habiting perfectly in both worlds. Mrs. Ramsay was purely domesticated, as was Julia Stephen. The house is a symbol of security, away from the din of social life. Virginia Woolf portrayed the symbol of the house very vividly because of the stability it affords amidst the flux of life, similar to the lighthouse amidst the ever-moving sea. A symbolic dimension making Mrs. Ramsay feel that "Others will come back to this night; this moon, this wind, this house; and to her too." (175)

In an effort to portray his father's intellectual personality, Andrew describes the kitchen table. The design on the table-cloth appeals to Lily's artistic sensibility, "to feel simply that's a chair, that's a table, and yet at the same time, it's a miracle, it's an ecstasy." (310) Mrs. Ramsay's dinner party is symbolic in nature. It symbolizes her creativity, physically and emotionally. The "Boeuf en Daube" was a great success and on the other hand was her invisible hand of grace creating harmony in disunity. It is like the Christmas dinner at the Dedalus household, projecting a catalogue of feelings and emotions of the participants: "Nothing need be said: nothing could be said. There it was, all round them. It partook . . . of eternity." (158)

Hermione Lee says about Mrs. Ramsay: "few others can resist her power, particularly at the dinner party, where she appears as a pagan deity presiding over a sacrificial rite in which Paul and Minta are the Victims."[59]

The novel commences on a literary plane—Mrs. Ramsay is seen reading to her youngest son James. For Ramsay, Scott's novels expose a great deal of human experience. In the final scene, Mr. Ramsay closes his novel, with a triumphant thrill. Intellectuals had no place in Mrs. Ramsay's affections, since she preferred boobies like Paul Rayley to intellectuals like Tansley. But books did appeal to her, as did the literary conversation at the dining table: "She let it uphold her and sustain her, this admirable fabric of the masculine intelligence." (159) After dinner, while reading a Shakespearean sonnet, Mrs. Ramsay experienced a moment of revelation:

> She was climbing up those branches, this way and that; laying hands on one flower and then another.
>
> Nor praise the deep vermilion in the rose,
>
> she read, and so reading she was ascending, she fled, on to the top, on to the summit. How satisfying! How restful! All the odds and ends of the day stuck to this magnet; her mind felt swept, felt clean. And then there it was, suddenly entire shaped in her hands, beautiful and reasonable, clear and complete, the essence sucked out of life and held rounded here—the Sonnet. (181-82)

Katharine Hilbery had a similar experience while walking with Ralph Denham—a feeling of oneness, peace and serenity.

The lighthouse is the central symbol depicting Mr. Ramsay's essential loneliness, Mrs. Ramsay's emotional fulfilment by identifying herself with its third beam and generally implying the flux and stability of life—signified by the solid structure surrounded by perpetual flux of water. Water, sea and waves indicate the mood and experiences of the characters. The sea-imagery pervades the three novels, *The Voyage Out, To the Lighthouse* and *The Waves*, where it forms the very structure on which the narratives are based. The depth of the sea fathoms the depths of Mrs. Ramsay's inner being. Cam's meditation is strewn with the mysticism the sea holds for her:

> They don't feel a thing there, Cam thought, looking at the shore, which rising and falling became steadily more distant and more peaceful. Her hand cut a trail in the sea, as her mind made the green swirls and streaks into patterns and, numbed and shrouded, wandered in imagination in that underworld of waters where the pearls stuck in clusters to white sprays, where, in the green light a change came over one's entire mind and one's body shone half transparent enveloped in a green cloak. (30)

For Mrs. Ramsay, the sea created varied sensations. The sound of the waves can be like a ghostly roll of drums "remorselessly beating the measure of life" (30) or like a "measured and soothing tattoo to her thoughts" and repeat consolingly "I am guarding you—I am your support." Similarly animal skulls play a very important part in most of her novels.

In *To the Lighthouse,* the boar's skull kept in the nursery terrifies the children and Mrs. Ramsay covers it with her shawl. In *Jacob's Room,* we find Jacob fascinated by a sheep's skull. This has an autobiographical basis, since Woolf's brother Thoby had once found a cow's skull while playing with Vanessa when they were little children. The autobiographical element is the essence of this book because the author has narrated her own experiences, has portrayed her parents and other family members, inculcating life and soul into the narrative:

> The presence of my mother obsessed me. I could hear her voice, see her, imagine what she would do or say as I went about my day's doings. She was one of the invisible presences who after all play so important a part in every life.[60]

In the year 1882, as told by John Lehmann in his book *Virginia Woolf and Her World,* Leslie Stephen bought Talland House at St. Ives which was annually visited as long as Julia was alive. This was a real treat for the children with unabounding pleasures of boating, fishing, playing on the sea-shore and watching the incessant flashing of the Godrevy Lighthouse.

Helen Ambrose, Mrs. Hilbery and Mrs. Ramsay were the prototypes of Virginia Woolf's mother Julia Stephen. Mrs. Ramsay possessed a sympathetic understanding and intuitive nature while Mr. Ramsay was an intellectual, rational and demanding individual turning to his wife for sympathy and encouragement. Mrs. Ramsay like Julia Stephen pitied men for this reason. Self-pity predominates the male intellectuals like St. John Hirst, Tansley and Mr. Ramsay who are the antithesis of the sensitivity, beauty and intuitive knowledge of their female counterparts:

> Nothing would make Mr. Ramsay move on. There he stood, demanding sympathy.
>
> Mrs. Ramsay, who had been sitting loosely, folding her son in her arm braced herself, and, half turning seemed to raise herself with an effort, and at once to pour erect into the air a rain of energy, a column of spray, looking at the same time animated and alive as if all her energies were being fused into force, burning and illuminating (quietly though she sat, taking up her stocking again), and into this delicious fecundity, this fountain and spray of life, the fatal sterility of the male plunged itself like a beak of brass, barren and bare. He wanted sympathy. He was a failure, he said. (61-62)

This passage augurs the relationship of Mr. and Mrs. Ramsay in the novel, as it was for Leslie and Julia Stephen.

When Mrs. Ramsay dies, Prue who was in reality Stella Duckworth, Julia Stephen's daughter, manages the home. She, like Stella, died in childbirth. Mr. Ramsay harassed them all as Sir Leslie did his wife Julia.

Virginia Woolf loved her beautiful, ethereal mother and loved her father only for his intellectual abilities. Like James, she hated him for persistently imposing himself on her mother. A note from her diary:

> Father's birthday. He would have been ninety-six, today, and could have been ninety-six like other people one has known, but mercifully was not. His life would have entirely ended mine. What would have happened? No writing, no books—inconceivable.
>
> I used to think of him and mother daily, but writing "The Lighthouse" laid them in my mind. And now he comes back sometimes but differently (I believe this to be true—that I was obsessed by them both, unhealthy; and writing of them was a necessary act). He comes back more as a contemporary. I

> must read him some day. I wonder if I can feel again, I hear his voice, I know this by heart?

Bankes envisions her in an archetypal association: "Greek, blue-eyed, straight-nosed. . . . The Graces assembling seemed to have joined hands in meadows of ashphodel to compose that face." (50) She is the instrument for maintaining peace and harmony in her home. She had to constantly adjust to her husband's demanding nature and soothe his tension-ridden nerves, from continuous assault on her peace. It was an indecipherable silence, portrayed on the lines of her mother wherein her sensitivity was shielded from pain and sorrow, a sphere of confidence in this nebulous world. Her love for children and her complete diffusion with their beings, her merry involvement in their fun and games, synthesized her imaginative nature with those of the children:

> Often she found herself sitting and looking, with her work in her hands until she became the thing she looked at—that light for example . . . she praised herself in praising the light without vanity, for she was stern, she was searching, she was beautiful like that light. (95)

This pure, innocent and simple woman was instantly loved by children, but she could never identify herself with her husband's academic jargon. She communed more easily with nature and her own imaginative world. The whole novel is created as a halo surrounding Mrs. Ramsay, dazzling the people and providing solace to the people around her with the beams of her personality, a perfect androgynous symbol. The feminine principle pervades the narration with its serenity, with all the other characters directing their vision towards a single point, making her spiritually invincible. In solitude, she was like a rose-bud:

> Mrs. Ramsay seemed to fold herself together, one petal closed in another; and the whole fabric fell in exhaustion upon itself, so that she had only strength enough to move her finger, in

> exquisite abandonment to exhaustion, across the page of Grimm's fairy story, while there throbbed through her, like the pulse in a spring which has expanded to its full width and now gently ceases to beat, the rapture of successful creation. (54)

Mr. Ramsay, with all his intellect and philosophy is basically a man of simplicity, leading a simple life and happy even with a meal of bread and cheese. He is a straightforward man harbouring no illusions of life. He visualizes himself as a promontory eaten away by the sea. Storms, shipwrecks and deaths have been woven together along with his transient fame to portray life. Thus he is introduced on a note of dissonance. He is ruthlessly truthful and possessed a very stubborn nature. It is only with equanimity that his wife absolves all tensions, penetrating the crude exterior and soothing him till he is peaceful and tranquil again. He could never decipher his wife's personality, but he loved her and worshipped her beauty. In reality he was a complex and lonely individual. His attempt to marshal knowledge under an alphabetical order proves his metaphysical bent of mind. Metaphysical aspects are concerned with the materialistic and the sensory worlds of existence. Virginia Woolf integrated this concept in her theory of androgyny. She has also delineated a rationalist Mr. Ramsay, who metamorphoses into a man of fine sensibility. This is a slow process of transformation since the ensuing damage had already been incurred on the other family members. His austerity, his consistent demand for truth and discipline and antagonistic behaviour disrupts all relationships especially an amiable and companionable relationship with his children. At times,like Mrs. Ramsay, he too could discard vanity and project his inner being:

> It was his power, his gift, suddenly to shed all superfluities, to shrink and diminish so that he looked barer and felt sparer, even physically, yet lost none of his intensity of mind, and so to stand on his little hedge facing the dark of human experience, how we know nothing and the sea eats away the ground

we stand on—that was fate, his gift . . . not only fame but even his own name was forgotten by him, he kept even in that desolation a vigilance which spared no phantom and luxuriated no vision. (72)

Marder explicates on the final landing at the lighthouse:

> Mr. Ramsay's landing on the rock is a symbol of illumination; it stands for a unity of being that can be attained only now and then by the rare individual wrestling with his soul. It is an experience that takes place in solitude, and, as the crucial moment of "To The Lighthouse" approach, we are reminded of Mr. Ramsay's essential loneliness, in spite of the shadowy presence of his children. It is a mystery that transcends the temporal order; the solitary old man seems to be leaping in space.[62]

Lily Briscoe is synonymous with Virginia Woolf. She is the person from whom radiates the impressions of Mrs. Ramsay, the principal consciousness. Her thought-processes convey a lot of depth to the narrative. An intelligent girl deals with a motley combination of characters adroitly. She is a devoted artist keeping marriage in abeyance which would have obtruded her artistic vision. Her art revolves round space and is portrayed on the lines of impressionist artists like Cezanne, Roger Fry and others. "The still space that lies about the heart of things, where one could move or not," (163) a region to be explored, because it is an essential format of the human psyche. Her painting is not only an aesthetic fulfilment but also an emotional fulfilment because it was an imaginative expression for Mrs. Ramsay which even memory could not substantiate. Lily feels unreal-like though she steps off her "strip of board into the waters of annihilation." (205) She imagines reality and eternal truth in the small fixities of life, like a company of gnats, each embodied separately but "marvellously controlled in an invisible elastic net."

Leon Edel writes about delineating real emotions in words:

"As a snow flake crystal caught in the warm hand is no longer a crystal but a drop, so, instead of catching a feeling of relation moving to its term, we find we have caught some substantive thing."[63] While painting, Woolf tries to capture her personal vision, reality and truth of life:

> Mrs. Ramsay bringing them together, Mrs. Ramsay saying "life stand still here": Mrs. Ramsay making of the moment something permanent (as in another sphere Lily herself tried to make of the moment something permanent)—this was of the nature of a revelation. In the midst of chaos there was shape; this eternal passing and flowing (she looked at the clouds going and the leaves shaking) was struck into stability. Life stand still here, Mrs. Ramsay said, " Mrs. Ramsay! Mrs. Ramsay!" she repeated. She owed this revelation to her. (240)

Lily was in a dilemma, concerning her artistic vision. She envisioned the aesthetic beauty of her surroundings but was unable to transfix it realistically with her medium. Her attempt to relate superficial and inner beauty within the ordinariness of life was her intense desire. But in the final scene, her being is pervaded with a sensation of peace and harmony. She is finally able to penetrate the external beauty of Mrs. Ramsay and have a glimpse of the eternal beauty of her soul. She overcomes her complexities and sympathizes with Mrs. Ramsay. Finally she triumphantly portrays her elusive vision on canvas dissolving all dissonance pervaded with peace and tranquillity. Meanwhile, the boat which carries Mr. Ramsay and others touches the opposite shore of the lighthouse. Thus this is the moment of inspiration for Lily Briscoe. A momentary revelation enables her to complete her painting in a single stroke. As Suzanne Langer says, "the more barren and indifferent the symbol, the greater its semantic power."[64]

> She looked at the steps; they were empty, she looked at her canvas; it was blurred. With a sudden intensity as if she saw

it clear for a second, she drew a line there, in the centre." (310)

Maria Di Battista says that the novel, like *The Winter's Tale,* concludes in the Heurisis or "finding again"[65] of the mother by the daughter. The mother who has cast a "triangular shadow over the step" (274) is reëmbodied and restored to life in the work of art through which is built up a whole structure of the imagination. (68)

Yet the work of art itself expresses more than this genealogical affinity between Mrs. Ramsay's fecundity and Lily's creative powers. Lily's picture represents the novel's completed effort to reconcile antithetical visions of reality. It captures the light of a butterfly's wing—the beauty of the world wrought by the fecund feminine will—burning on a framework of steel.

James is introduced to us on a note of dualism—serenely playing near his mother and we see his intense rage on seeing his father. This Oedipus complex would be discarded only in the final scene on the boat, with only two encouraging words of his father—"well done." He had inherited his mother's gentle sensibility, which she was so proud of and attempted to protect from her husband's crude dominating behaviour. William Bankes was a centre of consciousness outside the family. Apparently, he was deceptively simple. His friend Mr. Ramsay had successfully established a family, unlike him. He had developed cold, detached and at times critical mannerisms. Tansley created a hostile atmosphere with his rude and antagonistic behaviour, suffering from an inferiority complex rooted in his poverty-stricken childhood. He was a scholar and a great admirer of Mr. Ramsay.

Virginia Woolf may have been an agnostic but a vein of Christianity does run through her narratives. William Tindall is of the opinion that the lighthouse represents God, Death, Eternity and the Absolute, and that it is the goal of all endeavours.[66] Cam's two birds sitting outside a tree of Mrs. Ramsay's room are named by Lee as Mary and Joseph. (168) On reflection, Mrs. Ramsay envisaged her strip of life, constituting of fifty years:

There it was before her life. Life: She thought but she did not

> finish her thought. She took a look at life, for she had a clear sense of it there, something real, something private, which she shared neither with her children, nor with her husband. A sort of transaction went on between them in which she was on one side, and life was on another, and she was always trying to get the better of it as it was of her. (118)

But Mrs. Ramsay's involvement with herself was only a fraction compared to that of Mrs. Dalloway who was wholly imbued with life, her own sphere of existence, with nothing much in common with her husband and daughter. But Mrs. Ramsay was totally involved with her family except a few isolated moments of joyful communion in silence with nature or life.

> To be silent: to be alone. All the being and the doing, expansive, glittering, vocal, evaporated; and one shrunk, with a sense of solemnity, to being oneself, a wedge-shaped core of darkness, something invisible to others. (94)

Her scene of reconciliation with life is when she triumphs over flux and time. Virginia Woolf too sought truth and reality from this indecipherable mass of humanity through the medium of her art, injecting life into the sodden lumps of colour. Mrs. Ramsay's beautiful, philosophical sensibility was sufficient to draw out the pearl from the oyster. She required no medium to transmit her sensations. N.C. Thakur analyzes her personality in philosophical terms, "In contrast with the analytical Mr. Ramsay who cannot see Z-symbol of reality—Mrs. Ramsay's sitting in forgetfulness, like Yen Hai, is capable of that which Henri Bergson calls "l'experience integral," In a state of "Samadhi"—transcendental consciousness—Mrs. Ramsay sees "a coherence of things, a stability;" something that "in the face of the flowing, the fleeting the spectral" shines like a ruby, (163) and Lily Briscoe realizes that "in the midst of chaos" there is shape, and that "this eternal passing and flowing (is) struck into stability" (249): "This suggests that intuition alone is capable of what the Indian Yogis call 'anubhava'—integral experience—and the Zen Buddhists name 'Satori'—enlightenment—and thus confirms what Pascal says: the heart has its reasons of which the reason knows nothing."[67] On the return of her extra-corporeal spirit for a short while, normalcy is regained, the union of certain spirits takes place and certain souls gain peace by her spiritual and beneficent powers.

Mrs. Ramsay could never decipher the ugly, academic jargon of erudites like Tansley and desperately focusses her attention outside this sphere of ugly egoism, and intrinsically united with the beams of the lighthouse, instead of listening to his high-flown dialectic. When her husband stood near-by demanding sympathy, and James sitting on her lap silently appealing for her love and protection, she gave her all to them and did not leave a fraction of anything for herself. She even improved her own outlook of life from the viewpoints of her children.

T.E. Apter says, "The extension of Mrs. Ramsay's own consciousness, rests upon her sympathy with the consciousness of others. She grants to others a reality, which usually in Virginia Woolf's works is seen to be achieved only in isolation."[68] Margaret Crossland discussing the modern women novelists describes Mrs. Ramsay as the focal point of her household and everyone turns to her as the sunflower to the sun. Her social conscience was all-pervasive and she died having lavished and spent her being in the cause of her social responsibilities. Her death is a protest on behalf of all womankind.[69]

According to Lily, Mrs. Ramsay had suffered from a mania for matchmaking since she presided with immutable calm over destinies which she completely failed to understand. (81) She had played the role of the unifier, exercising her philanthropy over the children, creating communication between people around her. Her dinner party is a perfect example of her creativity and a social code which is able to harmonize polarities of varied consciousness especially of men who are socially sterile and require a feminine touch to steer them along. Mrs. Ramsay's divine power radiates peace and tranquillity all around. Her visionary insight appealed to Lily and Carmichael, who were themselves endowed with fine sensibilities.

But she could not traverse on the path of life similar to that of her husband because this rational being was a contradiction to her powerful interaction with nature. Even in this polaristic relationship, being spiritually isolated from him, she respects him "a great mind like his must be different." (112)

Her social consciousness does not allow any impediment or regression in social communication. When there was tension between Lily and Tansley at the dinner table Mrs. Ramsay's reaction was extreme:

> I am drowning, my dear, in seas of fire. Unless you apply some balm to the anguish of this hour and say something nice to that young man there, life will run upon the rocks. (138)

During the dinner, she felt as though she brought together this "house full of unrelated passions" under her aegis and then drifts back to her private world, shedding her superficial garb and stepping back to perceive her creation.

Man lives in a world of contingency and finitude. The modern psychological novelists have succeeded in transcending the temporal and spatial limitations. The only impasse for them is death which means the elimination of a personality from the face of the earth. But the spirit abounds and is eternal and all-pervasive and can never be conquered. This is the only factor which binds man's consciousness to finite levels and roots out any elements of vanity or egoism. Death cannot be surmounted by any force. William Barrett's impression on reading Tolstoy's *The Death of Ivan Ilyitch,* "Modern man has lost the meaning of life and it will take nothing less than the presence of death to restore this sense of life."[70]

Virginia Woolf's approach to death has taken a mystical turn. In *Mrs. Dalloway*, the curtain flutters by the wind and the birds of Paradise appear to come alive, as though Septimus himself has come into the room. Lily experiences a similar mystical experience after Mrs. Ramsay's death. While attempting to complete the picture she had commenced ten years ago, she distinctly sees her shadowlike figure through a window. Death-consciousness has a central place in Woolf's narratives. Similarly, in Saul Bellow's *Mr. Sammler's Planet*, the protagonist lives the experience of death continually, as does Septimus Smith. Virginia Woolf had written away her obsession, a necessary cathartic acting for her psychological well-being, a spiritual act in the intervening space between life and death.

A Haunted House is a revelation of a treasure buried in the precincts of the soul, referred to as "the light in the heart."[71] Similarly, Abbie Finlay writes, "The one factor deduced from an elegy is the light out of darkness," in his book *The Elegiac Mode*.

Mr. Ramsay's character is individualistic but Mrs. Ramsay's consciousness pervades the characters in the novel in a diffused manner being identifiable with her environment and the world around her. The author rediscovered her mother and this spiritual freedom, free from a persistent constriction of her soul which continued to have free reign in her remaining novels. Memories of her mother haunted her subconscious which she vaguely deciphered, as we perceive in this diary entry:

> Yet I am now and then haunted by some semi-mystic very profound life of a woman, which shall all be told on one occasion; and time shall be utterly obliterated, future shall somehow blossom out of the past. Once incident say the fall of a flower—might contain it.[72]

The conclusion of the novel is very significant because the consciousnesses of the protagonists undergo a complete transformation. It appears as though a supernatural power has directed a radiant beam transfiguring their mental beings into illuminated objects, with peace and serenity pervading all around. Mr. Ramsay underwent a drastic transition from an intellectual to an intuitive soul. James and Cam learnt to love and accept their father. Lily achieved her artistic goal and a contentment with a momentary vision, fulfilling any desire she ever had. Mrs. Ramsay with her invisible presence achieved what was her continual effort to spread peace and harmony to all mankind. The synthesis was complete by the synaesthetic moment envisioned by Lily.

NOTES

1. *A Writer's Diary,* 26th January 1930, p. 23.
2. Hermione Lee, *The Novels of Virginia Woolf* (London: Methuen, 1977), p. 90.
3. Virginia Woolf, *Jacob's Room* (London: Hogarth Press, 1960), p. 89.
4. Virginia Woolf, *Moments of Being,* ed. Jeane Schulkind (London: Hogarth Press, 1978), p. 20.
5. Virginia Woolf, "The Death of the Moth," *Collected Essays* (New York: Harcourt Brace, 1942), p. 360.
6. W.Y. Tindall, *The Literary Symbol* (New York: Columbia University Press, 1955), pp. 140-41.
7. A.H. Maslow, "Frustration, Threat and Deprivation," *Psychological Review, 48, 364, 1941.*
8. *Moments of Being,* p. 125.
9. T.S. Eliot, Holograph Note Book Berg Collection, Public Library, New York.
10. Robert Ornstein, *The Nature of Human Consiousness: A Book of Readings* (San Francisco, W.H. Freeman, 1968), p. 5.
11. Avrom Fleishman, *Virginia Woolf: A Critical Reading* (Baltimore: John Hopkins University Press, 1975), p. 58.
12. T.E. Apter, p. 49.
13. Leon Edel, *The Psychological Novel* (London: Rupert Hart-Davis, 1972), p. 18.
14. Virginia Woolf, *Roger Fry: A Biography* (New York: Harcourt Brace, 1940), p. 172.
15. Quentin Bell, *Virginia Woolf: A Biography* (London: The Hogarth Press, 1972), I, p. 125.
16. Jean O. Love, pp. 146-47.
17. Virginia Woolf, *Mrs. Dalloway* (London: The Hogarth Press, 1925).
18. Avrom Fleishman, pp. 70-71.
19. Georges Poulet, *The Interior Distance,* trans. Elliot Coleman (Baltimore: John Hopkins University Press, 1959), p. 16.
20. John Graham, "Time in the Novels of Virginia Woolf," *University of Toronto Quarterly,* Vol. 18, 1949, p. 186.
21. Jean O. Love, p. 150.

22. William Shakespeare, *Cymbeline*, Act 4, Sc. 2.
23. William Shakespeare, *Othello*, Act 2, Sc. 1.
24. L. Heinz and A. Rowena, *The Individual Psychology of Alfred Adler* (London: George Allen and Unwin, 1988), pp. 47-48.
25. Mitchell S. Leaska, *The Novels of Virginia Woolf: From Beginning to End*, p. 100.
26. Herbert Marder, *Feminism and Art: A Study of Virginia Woolf* (Chicago: University of Chicago Press, 1968), p. 94.
27. Alaine Robbe-Grillet, *Snapshots and Towards a New Novel*, trans. Barbara Wright (London, 1965), p. 138.
28. *A Writer's Diary*, 14th October, 1922, p. 52.
29. *Ibid.*, 19th June 1923, p. 57.
30. Leonard Woolf, *Beginning Again: An Autobiography of the Years 1911-1981* (London: The Hogarth Press, 1964), pp. 76-77.
31. L. Heinz and A. Rowena, p. 244.
32. R.D.Laing, "Divided Self," *Virginia Woolf s Mrs. Dalloway—A Study in Alienation*, ed. Jeremy Hawthorne (London: Chatto and Windus, 1975).
33. *A Writer's Diary*, Saturday, Feb. 18th, 1923, p. 51.
34. *Ibid*, Saturday, August 2nd, 1924, p. 68.
35. W.Y. Tindall, pp. 98-99.
36. *Ibid.*, p. 202.
37. Alan Kennedy , p. 17.
38. Avrom Fleishman, pp. 88-89.
39. *A Writer's Diary*, Saturday, December 13th, 1924, p. 74.
40. *Ibid.*, p. 65.
41. Yuri Borev, *Aesthetics: The Sociology of Art* (Moscow: Progress Publishers, 1985), p. 56.
42. *Ibid.*, p. 98.
43. *Ibid.*, p. 100.
44. David Daiches, *Virginia Woolf* (Norfolk, Connecticut: New Direction Books, 1942), p. 86f.
45. Herbert Marder, p. 138.
46. Mitchell Leaska, *The Novels of Virginia Woolf: From Beginning to End*, p. 145.
47. D.H. Lawrence, *Fantasia of the Unconsciousness and Psychoanalysis of the Unconscious* (London: William Heinemann, 1961), p. 208.
48. Bernard Blackstone, *Virginia Woolf: A Commentary* (London: The Hogarth Press, 1949), p. 82.

49. *A Writer's Diary*, 14th May 1925, p. 75.
50. *Ibid.*, Saturday, 27th June 1925, p. 83.
51. Virginia Woolf, *To the Lighthouse* (London: The Hogarth Press, 1927), pp. 151-52.
52. Victor G. Panov, *Emotions, Myths and Theories*, trans. H.Campbell Creighton (Moscow: Progress Publishers, 1985), p. 15.
53. V.I. Lenin, *Materialism and Empiro-Criticism* (Moscow: Progress Publishers, 1977), p. 111.
54. Josephine O'Brien Schaefer, p. 73.
55. *A Writer's Diary*, Friday, 30th April 1926.
56. John Graham, pp. 186-201.
57. A.B. Goldenveizer, "Talks with Tolstoy," trans. A.B. Kotelianksy and Virginia Woolf (1923), pp. 91-94, in James Hafley, *The Creative Modulation of Perspective* (1954).
58. Ernst Cassirer, *The Philosophy of Symbolic Forms* (New Haven: Yale University Press, 1953), p. 85.
59. Hermione Lee, p. 129.
60. *Moments of Being*, p. 93.
61. *A Writer's Diary*, 28th November 1928, p. 138.
62. Herbert Marder, p. 153.
63. Leon Edel, p. 20.
64. Suzanne K. Langer, *Philosophy in a New Key: A Study in the Symbolism of Reason, Rite and Art* (New York: Charles Scribner, 1953), p. 75.
65. Maria Di Battista, *Virginia Woolf s Major Novels—The Fables of Anon* (London: Yale University Press, 1980), p. 107.
66. Carl Woodring, *Virginia Woolf* (New York: Columbia University Press, 1966), p. 23.
67. Quoted from N.C. Thakur, *The Symbolism of Virginia Woolf* (London: Oxford University Press, 1965), p. 78.
68. T.E. Apter, p. 95.
69. Margaret Crossland, *Beyond the Lighthouse: English Women Novelists in the Twentieth Century* (New York: Taplinger, 1981), p. 25.
70. William Barrett, *Existentialism as a Symptom of Man's Contemporary Crisis: Spiritual Problems in Contemporary Literature*, ed. Stanley Romaine Hopper (New York, 1952), p. 143.
71. Virginia Woolf, *A Haunted House and Other Stories* (London: The Hogarth Press, 1944), p. 270.
72. *A Writer's Diary*, Tuesday, 23rd November 1926, p. 104.

The Conflicting Self

In *Jacob's Room*, *Mrs. Dalloway* and *To the Lighthouse*, Virginia Woolf has dealt with one absorbing problem: the necessity to reconcile divergent personalities within marriage and the syntheses of the individual consciousness with the group-mentality. She comes to the conclusion that there is no final solution. In *Orlando*, she tries to escape from the problems of present-day life. She therefore retreats into the fantasy-biography. The escape is provided by a whimsical accentuation of the Tiresias motif which has already appeared in *Mrs. Dalloway*. By utilizing the pageant device and the backdrop of history Virginia Woolf reiterates some of her favourite themes like the attic room of *Night and Day* and *Mrs Dalloway*, the longing for the Turkish hills in *Jacob's Room* and the house which is a main character in *To the Lighthouse*. Virginia Woolf manages to recreate the changing spirit of English history and the English way of life through the metamorphosis of a single individual.

The sub-title, "a Biography," reflects Virginia Woolf's desire to write about an individual. Earlier, she had successfully written in a similar vein about Elizabeth Barrett Browning from the perspective of her dog Flush and also a posthumous record of Roger Fry. *Orlando* and *Flush* are intermingled with ironical references where their pitiable conditions are satirized. *To the Lighthouse* was a direct biography of her family, which was to recreate the spirits of her parents which had always haunted her. *Orlando* is a pageant of the nobility, a star-spangled life of the rich wherein the author's beloved friend Victoria Sackville-West dominates the whole proceedings. Their relationship was on an intimate plane and Virginia Woolf was acquainted with Vita's extreme sensitivity towards her ancestral home Knole. But being born a woman, she was denied the right of inheritance. This pain Virginia Woolf attempted to disseminate through her imagination. Through literary allusions she fused facts and illusion, weaving a narrative which was widely acclaimed.

Vita Sackville-West was a novelist who won the Hawthornden Prize for her poem *The Land.* Her two novels *The Heir* and *The Edwardians* have references to manor houses similar to Knole. Hermione Lee has concisely mentioned these references in her book. In *The Heir,* sub-titled *A Love Story,* a quiet little man from Wolverhampton suddenly finds himself in possession of a Kentish Elizabethan manor house. The story describes his increasingly possessive love for the place, which is heavily mortgaged and has to be auctioned. The hero Chase, finds the thought of losing the house more and more unbearable, for "The house was the soul and did contain and guard the soul as in a casket . . . the soul of England."[1] Virginia Woolf was aware of this historical background and the intensity of Vita's emotional involvement with the grandiose mansion. By inculcating her theory of androgyny and stretching the narrative over a span of thirty years she accomplished, though only in fiction, what her friend Vita had desired to possess in her ancestral home. As David Daiches says about *Orlando:* "It would be a weary talk to disentangle the profoundly symbolic from the deliberately irresponsible."[2]

Avrom Fleishman remarks on the establishment of the esthetic mode which helps to build up a literary atmosphere:

> *Orlando* is a literary biography not merely in recounting the life and times of a writer but in transforming that account into literature itself—making her biography a literary object which is her adequate symbol.[3]

Orlando synthesizes through literature what Vita Sackville-West's sensibility could do as a writer and it brings together the literary experience of her ancestors. The plot is made fantastic by the sex transformation of Orlando when he is thirty-years old. It is a transfusion of his psychic life by combining the two sexual forces at the advent of the eighteenth century. Orlando is the best example of Virginia Woolf's determination to give all things their caricature-value especially the exaggerated, ruthless interpretation of the dominant comic theme—human sexuality. Sex confusion is the prime topic of comedy in dramatizing the conflict between the instinctual self and the civilized, conventional world it must negotiate in.

The plot is systematically divided into six parts with direct reference to the history of the Sackvilles, including Vita's gypsy grandmother. In Virginia Woolf's earlier books, marriage has been an intense involvement, an institution for adjustment and reconciliation. But in this fantasy-ridden novel, marriage, like Orlando's marriage to Rosina Pepita, is only a requisite for existence in society. Orlando's marriage to Bonthrop Marmaduke Shelmerdine is for an intense desire for companionship and to legitimize her child which she conceived in one of her romantic interludes.

In the present novel, Woolf has deviated from the traditional style altogether and to a certain degree from the technique of *Jacob's Room, Mrs. Dalloway* and *To the Lighthouse,* especially in the context of the time factor, and the element of parody, which pervade her novel: "We shape our thoughts till they become, the thinnest integument for our thoughts. Thoughts are divine."[4] Woolf tackles the subtle and elusive problems with flair and courage, making it an extremely pleasurable reading. Her style varies with the prerequisite ages with lyricism and this light vein carries the narrative to the end successfully. Her beautiful and descriptive language, each word gleaming like a precious stone, woven into the fabric of the narrative, the scenes depicting the spirit of the ages are like designs on a tapestry rendering the story in a realistic manner. It was difficult to interweave the two sexes embodied in a single individual and "often it has been necessary to speculate, to surmise, and even to make use of the imagination." (119) As the author herself professes in the novel, we notice the stylistic developments over the various periods she deals with. The passage quoted is in the context of Orlando's effort at a literary venture throughout the book: "The Oak Tree":

> For it is for the historian of letters to remark that he had changed his style amazingly. His floridity was chastened, his abundance curbed, the age of prose was congealing those warm fountains. (113)

On perusing the author's diary, we can evince her ideas of the novel which she planned in "a mock style very clear and plain,"[6] or it was meant to be "half laughing, half serious with great splashes of exaggeration."[7]

Virginia Woolf had written a criticism on a fresco by Perugino even before she had attempted her first novel which is quoted by Quentin Bell:

> I attain a different kind of beauty, achieve a symmetry by means of infinite discords, showing all the traces of the mind's passages through the world; achieve in the end, some kind of whole made of shivering fragments; to me this seems the natural process, the flight of the mind.[8]

This is the very same technique she applies in *Orlando:* innumerable disparate elements and extremely polaristic facts like the feminine and masculine sexes. The "shivering fragments" of her ideas are woven into a many-splendoured story, reflecting her percipient mind and mastery of rhetoric.

Orlando is a biographical extravaganza with a single thread interconnecting the various ages. "The Oak Tree," Orlando's poem, is indirectly related to Vita's poem *The Land.* We can visualize the changing mood of passing time, from masculine rationality to feminine romanticism, laced with feministic maltreatment. As in *Between the Acts*, English history is presented in a pageant form with Orlando as the protagonist. He is introduced in the Elizabethan age as a violent male, slashing away at a dehydrated Moor's head. The romantic Elizabethan era is represented by this handsome youth, sixteen years of age who loves solitude. The Queen is charmed by his beauty and innocence and confers on him the Order of the Garter. In the Jacobean age, his passionate affair with Sasha, the Russian ambassador's daughter is portrayed with the Great Forest of 1608 as the background. She betrays him and eventually, he leaves for Constantinople as the Ambassador of Great Britain. Here he secretly marries a gypsy, Rosina Pepita, and soon after falls into a week-long trance. On regaining consciousness he finds himself transformed into a woman. He lives with a band of gypsies for a short while and leaves for England during the eighteenth century. Unfortunately, Orlando has to face legal problems of inheritance due to his sexual transformation. Orlando busies herself with literary and social pursuits, meeting Pope, Swift and Addison in this era of wit and satire. The nineteenth century is introduced with limited enthusiasm:

> The great cloud which hung . . . on the first day of the nineteenth century stayed. . . . The sun shone, of course, but it was so girt about with clouds and the air was so saturated with water, that its beams were discoloured. (142)

Orlando discharges her duty as a woman, marries one Marmaduke Bonthrop Shelmerdine, bears a son in the Edwardian age. In the twentieth century, Shelmerdine returns from his voyage and "The Oak Tree" is completed and published.

Virginia Woolf's mastery of language projects to a great degree her original thoughts and feelings. This direct transcription of her beautiful sensibility is her greatest achievement. Providing her with an aesthetic fulfilment. This very emotional and literary process is portrayed in Lily Briscoe's artistic dilemma of her inability to transmute on canvas the picture in her mind. But she finally did achieve her desire when she had her vision. Virginia Woolf's language varies with the theme, a precious gift endowed on her. In *Orlando,* the language takes a tone of infinite grandeur, the translucence of timelessness, the strength of satire and a fabulous imagination to mould her fantasy:

> Birds froze in mid-air and fell like stones to the ground. At Norwich a young country woman started to cross the road in her usual robust health and was seen by the onlookers to turn visibly to powder and be blown in a puff of dust over the roofs as the icy blast struck her at the street corner. (21)

Virginia Woolf's multifaceted approach to time makes her novel interesting and thought-provoking. An ardent admirer of Chekhov, she pursues his style of life surrounded by space and time. In *Orlando* and *Between the Acts*, she projects time in a historical tone, with a similar background portraying the various spirits of the ages. In *Orlando*, her treatment of the time-factor is unique, in the manner in which she elongates and condenses the clock-time:

> . . . time, unfortunately, though it makes animals and vegetables bloom and fade with amazing punctuality, has no such simple effect upon the mind of man. The mind of man, moreover, works with equal strangeness upon the body of time. An hour, once it lodges in the queer element of the human spirit, may be stretched to fifty or a hundred times its clock-length; on the other hand, an hour may be accurately represented on the timepiece of the mind by one second. (91)

Woolf represents chronological time by clocks, as in St. Paul's, St. Margaret's and Big Ben. Memory is a conjoining factor interrelating the past and the present:

> Memory is a seamstress and a capricious one at that. Memory runs her needle in and out, up and down or what follows after. Thus, the most ordinary movement in the world, such as sitting down at a table and pulling the inkstand towards one, may agitate a thousand odd, disconnected fragments. (49)

We find Woolf's involvement with the past to be Proustian in nature.

Time is an important leitmotif in the modern psychological novels. In 1891, Henry Nicols wrote in a review on temporal experience:

> Casting an eye backward we can but be struck by the wide variety of explanation offered by the time mystery. Time has been called an act of mind or reason, of perception, of intuition; of sense, of memory, of will. . . . It has been deemed a general sense accompanying all mental content in a manner similar to that conceived by pain and pleasure. It has been assigned a separate special disparate sense, to a dozen kinds of "feeling," some familiar, some strangely invented for the difficulty. It has been explained by "struggles," by "luminous trains." . . . It has been declared a priori, innate, intuitive, empirical, mechanical. It has been deduced from within and without, from heaven and from earth.[9]

For example, Orlando is thirty-six years old according to chronological time and more than three hundred years old in inner time. This temporality corresponds to Bergson's inner duree and outer time. As a normal individual, Orlando has lived through four centuries. But the present moment in 1928 encompasses her past completely, disagreeing with the metaphor, that pre-history is deeper, grander, more sonorous than the present moment. Gillian Beer says that the novel holds the knowledge that cultures and histories are obliterated, that things may not endure.[10]

Since the autobiographical element has been seen to pervade all Woolf narratives, *Orlando* too contains a great deal of her biography: "In short, every secret of a writer's soul, every experience of his life, every quality of his mind is written large in his works." (189-90) It is as if Terence Hewet is speaking in *The Voyage Out.*

Virginia Woolf's early experiences triggered dual reactions in her—one was sexual frigidity with men and secondly, a good rapport with women. Beautiful and talented women like Vita aroused her sensibility. "The whole of *Orlando* is there to prove how passionately she could love a woman," comments Roger Poole.[11] Stephen Spender too feels that *Orlando* is "a fantastic meditation on a portrait of Vita Sackville-West."[12] Vita herself had written an article, including Virginia's letters to her, regarding the composition of *Orlando:*

> Suppose Orlando turns out to be Vita, and it's all about you and the lure of your mind—heart you have none—suppose there's the kind of shimmer of reality which sometimes attaches to my people as the lustre of an oyster shell . . . your excellence as a subject arises largely from your noble birth—but what's 400 years of nobility, all the same?—and the opportunity thus given for florid descriptive passages in great abundance.[13]

Virginia Woolf's continuous oneness with nature, triggered profound depth in her descriptive power. This rapport she portrays as the "English diseases," as termed by the gypsies in this novel. Virginia Woolf reflects Orlando's course of thoughts, a tapestry of nature embroidered with the love and desire of Apollo for Daphne. Nature is often a poet's muse for proliferation of his thoughts.

The grandeur of nobility can be projected in their full glory, by the dazzling and divine beauty of jewels. Jewels play an important role in *Orlando*, from the beginning to the end. Queen Elizabeth slips a ring around the finger of young Orlando, ordaining the course of fate. During the celebrations of his Dukedom, gold is strewn in many forms for decoration. Pearls and emeralds aided him to survive after his transformation, when amongst the gypsies and after her return to England. But jewels were the coronet of her beauty:

> Here! here! she cried, baring her breast to the moon (which now showed bright) so that her pearls glowed like the eggs of some vast moon-spider. The aeroplane rushed out of the clouds and stood over her head. It hovered above her. Her pearls burnt like a phosphorescent flare in the darkness. (295)

The ethereal feel of precious stones is described, the house of nobility being a treasure-house wherein they even made love:

> The day was hot; their loves had been active; they had fallen asleep among the rubies. (30)

Gems were emblems of love and beauty and their very means of interaction in society, its infinite hues and radiance reflecting different aspects of communion at varied levels.

Apart from Orlando who is the protagonist of the novel, minor characters are highly emphasized in various forms. In *Orlando*, Virginia Woolf personifies three graces—Purity, Modesty and Chastity. They are presented as three ladies of morality, but their demands are in vain, because there stood Orlando in all her beauteous glory—transformed to a woman. Virginia Woolf's variance of opinion with these women was similar to her uprooting the Angel in her home. A woman should not be enchained by false traditions like subservience to man but that every individual should possess "the strength of a man and a woman's grace." (20-21)

"The Oak Tree" is a leitmotif woven throughout the novel, representing all the centuries portrayed with their nuances and prevailing attitudes. Fame obstructs smooth movement of one's mind. Obscurity enshrouds an individual and allows his verse to flow unimpeded, like a wave returning to the body of the sea minus envy and spite. Orlando thus sought refuge under the oak tree, away from the complexities of worldly existence.

> He sighed profoundly and flung himself on the earth at the foot of the oak tree. He loved, beneath all this summer transiency, to feel the earth's spine beneath him; for such he took the hard root of the oak tree to be; or, for image followed image, it was the back of a great horse that he was riding; or the deck of a tumbling ship—it was anything indeed, so long as it was hard, for he felt the need of something which he could attach his floating heart to. . . . To the oak tree and as he lay

> there, gradually the flutter in and about him stilled itself. (20-21)

His individuality, complete oneness with nature and love for solitude are very apparent. Very often in the novel there is an account of an epiphanous moment experienced under the canopy of the sky with all nature to revel in silence.

Androgyny is a technique for Virginia Woolf for uniting warring contraries of life. James Naremore too opposes "the world of the self, the time-bound, landlocked every-day world of the masculine ego, of intellect and routine, to the world without a self—watery, emotional, erotic, generally associated with the female sensibility."[14]

Mircea Eliade in the essay "Mephistopheles and the Androgyne or the Mystery of the Whole" has dealt with Jungian theories of sexual archetypes, divine androgyny, bisexual cosmogony and ritual hermaphroditism:

> If we remember that transvestitism was very widespread at Carnival, the spring festivity of Europe, and also in certain agricultural ceremonies in India, Persia and other Asiatic countries, we realise the principal function of this rite; it is, to be brief, a coming out of one's self, a transcending of one's own historically-controlled situation and a recovering of an original situation, no longer human or historical, since it precedes the foundation of human society; a paradoxical situation impossible to maintain in profane time, in a historical epoch, but which is important to reconstitute periodically in order to restore, if only for a brief moment, the initial completeness, the intact source of holiness and power.[15]

Orlando of course gains experience and pleasure due to his transformation. Orlando's androgynous nature has been described in the course of the novel:

> For it was this mixture in her of man and woman, one being

> uppermost and then the other, that often gave her conduct an unexpected turn. The curious of her sex would argue, for example, if Orlando was a woman, how did she never take more than ten minutes to dress? . . . Still, she has none of the formality of a man, or a man's love of power. She is excessively tender hearted. She could not endure to see a donkey beaten or a kitten drowned. Yet . . . she could bring with the best and liked games of hazard . . . whether, then, Orlando was most man or woman, it is difficult to say. (120)

Virginia Woolf leaves this fact for analysis: "Let biologists and psychologists determine" (139) the status of her sex. Sasha, being a girl, appeared dressed as a boy and the Archduchess Harriot too had been masquerading as a man. These are superficially androgynous unlike Orlando and Shelmerdine. Bernard in *The Waves* says, "Nor do I always know if I am man or woman."[16]

The highest aim of the feminist movement, as Virginia Woolf saw it, was to prepare the way for profound adjustments in the inner lives of the sexes. A marriage had to be consummated, she said, within the mind itself of each individual, "a union between the masculine and feminine principles."[17] Androgyny is a means of existence, of survival, a compromise between the two sexes, which would subvert feminine tyranny and bring about universal harmony. *A Room of One's Own* was written at this time, dealing with androgyny and giving a historical account of the development of women down the ages, including an imaginary sister of Shakespeare. In *Orlando* too, we are given a picture of the extreme enjoyment and freedom enjoyed by men and the inhibited lives of women; thus the satire of the three sisters, Purity, Chastity and Modesty, to relegate women behind closed doors, and cringe under the rule of the dominant male. Feminist literature is widely published now and women have realized the folly of their subservient position in society. Catharine R. Stimpson in her article "Feminism and Feminist Criticism" has paid a tribute to women writers, seeking a dialectic improvement of the status of women:

> Since the late 1960s the meaning of being a feminist critic has deepened. It has, however, consistently entailed assuming the validity of a tough Parsimonious Theory: we cannot understand history, society or culture unless we graph the causes and effects of sex/gender systems. Such systems proliferate, foliate, and vary, but they have usually pushed down on women. Rochesters have bestrode the world more firmly, and freely, than Janes. Janes have had to choose between polishing their boots or declining to do so—at the risk of a kick. The feminist critic must break such sex/gender systems, using language as weapon and tool, and then labour to renew history, society, and culture.[18]

Caroline Heilbrun has described the members of the Bloomsbury Group as the first examples of the androgynous way of life: "they were all marvellously capable of love, that lust in their world was a joyful emotion, that jealousy and domination were remarkably sparse in their lives."[19] Maria di Battista projects this aspect in the context of Orlando who is in an emotional dilemma attempting to decipher the difference between poetry and truth. There is a contradiction between the violence of his desires and the tranquillity of art. Finally, Orlando comprehends the subtle relationship between desire and its artifices when she gazes at the antique tapestry depicting the legend of Daphne and Apollo, the God of poetry in pursuit of the Maiden fleeing from his embraces, the eternal round of poetry and desire.[20] Eroticism and the inspiration of the Muse are determined on a single plane of sensibility. Sasha's betrayal of his love and Greene's deception of their friendship did not disintegrate him emotionally but were a spring for the Muse. This was a necessary experience for Orlando, to inspire her for her literary pursuits and moral and aesthetic elevation.

The novel commences on a note of comical satire, with Orlando's mock-heroic chivalry of slicing the head of a Moor, long ago struck down by his ancestors. Virginia Woolf delineates Orlando's aristocratic features in a style befitting his nobility: "Orlando stood now in the midst of the yellow body of an heraldic leopard." (16) A consistent search for Orlando's true identity, within her home and her writing is visible, as Hermione Lee analyzes:

> the closest analogy between Orlando and her biographer is that both are struggling to find a way to expressing life (or truth, or reality: the terms are frequently interchangeable) in art. Orlando's attempts to write are, like her characters, partly evolved from and partly at odds with the historical periods through which she lives.[21]

The social self is subjective and spatial whereas the momentary self is our individual being and our real self. Orlando is portrayed through moving time, the historical-consciousness identifying with the personal-consciousness, signifying the two selves of an individual being—the true self and the captive self:

> She was . . . changing her selves as quickly as she drove . . . as happens when the conscious self which is the uppermost and has the power to desire, wishes to be nothing but oneself. This is what some people call the true self, and it is, they say, compact of all the selves we have it in us to be; commanded and locked up by the Captain self, the key self which amalgamates and controls them all. (219)

Orlando had to adjust emotionally too, with the transition of time. There were tremendous changes with the onset of every era and his various lifestyles. He was originally a young earl chosen by Queen Elizabeth to serve her. Then there is his passionate love-affair with Sasha during the Great Frost in the Jacobean age. In the literary field, Shakespeare and Marlowe were replaced by Donne and Sir Browne. Orlando himself had started writing poetry at the age of sixteen about Aethelbert, a tragedy in five acts with Vice, Crime and Misery as the enacting characters. In the reign of Charles II, he is an Ambassador to Constantinople. The pain of deception wrought by Sasha is replaced by an enlargement of spirit. He marries a gypsy but is metamorphosed to a woman. This emotional upheaval persists because of his uprooted lifestyle. The Duke now resides with the homeless gypsies. He returns to England in the Victorian era, only to face legal problems, a reflection of Vita's tragic loss of Knole having been born a woman. Orlando however bides over all complications and settles down with a husband and son in the nineteenth century, with motor cars and a mechanized life all around him. Thus she had to experience intense psychological changes which were borne with dignity and equanimity, befitting her noble birth. But memory is coeval to our thought-processes which can never be erased. Proust voiced similar ideas when he said that perceiving an individual is an "intellectual process" because the object perceived is a "transparent envelop" and a person is free to form any impression he has desired.[22] Orlando's emotions and feelings, since he was an extremely sensitive person with artistic inclination, climb a spiral stairway to the brain (17) and her mind is "a fluid that flowed round things and enclosed them." (23)

Orlando's infinite experience and discontinuous modes of existence are explained by R.L. Chambers as his theory of discontinuity of personality in which the self "consists not of a homogeneous entity capable of gathering experience to itself but rather of discrete moments of experience.[23]

Due to the metamorphosis, Orlando experiences characteristic psychological changes like the pleasure of resisting and yielding to masculine advances. Her former fearlessness and courage decimate to timidity and fear of ghosts, desiring their protection, swarthed in bales of crinoline. Orlando's life with the gypsies is stripped of her glamorous past. A luxurious lifestyle, with constant social interaction, was the position of the Ambassador representing the people of England. The beggarly, nomadic life was a complete contrast, an existence minus the gilded paraphernalia of robes and jewels. She has the sky as her roof overhead and nature as the four walls for a home. Life is transient and we should never be proud of our materialistic possessions which will ultimately turn to dust.

On escaping from the gypsies, Orlando continued to live amidst the aristocratic society of the eighteenth century when Pope,

Addison and Swift were in the top rungs of literary society. With her literary talents, her infinitely beautiful transaction with nature in the gypsy camp, and her capacity for diving into the innumerable lifestyles of the various ages, Orlando had the makings of a great writer. This reminds us of De Quincey's comparison of the human being to a Palimpsest:

> What else than a natural and mighty Palimpsest is the human brain? Such a Palimpsest . . . oh reader! is yours. Everlasting layers of ideas, images, feelings, have fallen upon your brain softly as light. Each succession has seemed to busy all that went before. And yet, in reality, not one has been extinguished.[24]

Orlando's androgynous mind raises her above the ordinary human beings. Her plane of consciousness being on a much higher strata than the rest. As such, social indictments and restraints did not figure in her dictionary and this of course is reflected in her biographer's state of mind. Elaine Showalter delineates the androgynous mind as the Utopian projection of an ideal artist:

> Calm, stable, unimpeded by consciousness of sex, Woolf meant it to be a luminous and fulfilling idea. . . . Her ideal artist mystically transcends sex, or has none . . . through total immersion in the individual experience.[25]

Orlando is a modern psychological novel, therefore its historical background has to be integrated to the present moment and Orlando's multi-faceted personality and creative spirit have to be congealed to a point to cater to present lifestyles as psychological necessity. Thus, the time-factor had to be synchronized, focussing on the triple aspects of time, space and personality. In this final present-moment of the twentieth century, the past and the present are encompassed into a united whole and we can feel Orlando's complete involvement with life, even with the infinite variations of her lifestyle.

Though Orlando derives joy in minor incidents but it was only in solitude that she could communicate with reality, with her unconscious being. Our real self can be evinced only in silence and solitude, the two inevitable factors which are pre-requisites to delve into our inner beings. We should have knowledge of ourselves to develop our personality and project our individuality. Therefore, Orlando gave prime importance to solitude and was not enamoured by societal contacts which held only limited meaning for her because in these superficial transactions, truth and reality were unknown. Virginia Woolf once spoke on the double-edged quality of society, of joy and pain, of man's dualistic nature, desiring solitude and company simultaneously on two planes of existence—the life of solitude and society. She writes in *A Room of One's Own,* "this astonishing precipice on one side of which the soul was active and in broad daylight, on the other side of which it was contemplative and dark as night." (165-66)

Orlando, having lived through both masculine and feminine roles, finds peace and harmony in her individual being. This was a harmonious state, free from patriarchal domination, with no spiritual or social quest since the universe was her home. The individual is thus perfectly integrated into society. In Jung's scheme of psychological notions, consciousness is a masculine domain and the unconsciousness the feminine principle. A woman therefore correlates with nature in an intimate manner due to her inherent intuitive being, a man diffuses perfectly with the upper crust of society, their rational intellectual beings helping in the interaction.

Virginia Woolf contradicted her father's theory that an artist should possess either a masculine or a purely feminine personality. Thus, her theory of androgyny was an important undercurrent in all her narratives. In *Orlando,* she could project her inner feelings by detracting from the normal technique of narrative style and adopting fantasy as her means of expression. She stresses the inner-being of her protagonist, her external activities being an extension of her subconscious love for freedom. Virginia Woolf sketches Orlando's character, either living with the gypsies or getting involved with a girl, imaginatively overstepping the emotional and physical boundaries destined for women. In *Women and Fiction,* she wrote that *Pride and Prejudice, Wuthering Heights, Villette* and *Middlemarch* were written by women from whom were withheld all experiences save that which could be met within a "middle-class drawing room."[26] In *Orlando,* Woolf had projected the Bloomsbury world into a humorous extravaganza as she used to do in her own conversation. There was much laughter in the final pages, indicating the prevailing of the biographer's satiric mood, regarding life and art. Bergson writes in *On Laughter in Comedy,* "there is something aesthetic about it, since the comic comes into being just when society and the individual, freed from worry of self-preservation, begin to regard themselves as works of art."[27]

Orlando was comfortable in solitude, so much so that she even felt close to death. In silence and solitude did a desire for death overcome her: "She said, 'I'm dead,' and pushed her way as a spirit might through the spectre-pale beech trees, and so oared herself deep into solitude as if the little flicker of noise and movement were over and she were free now to take her way." (162)

Virginia Woolf leaves us in great doubt about Orlando's feminity when she writes: "Truth compels us to say no . . . we may conclude that he or she is not better than a corpse and so leave her " (169) She then proceeds to explore life amidst the bird, the worm, the snail, and all nature itself, but her question is left unanswered. In the final pages of the book, Orlando finds herself in a quandary:

> Time had passed over her and an unsurmountable amount of memories had circulated, and she was unable to "synchronise the sixty or seventy different times which beat simultaneously." . . . But it is not altogether plain sailing . . . as Orlando said (being out in the country and needing another self presumably). Orlando? Still, the Orlando she needs may not come; these selves of which we are built up, one on top of another, as plates are piled on a waiter's hand, have attachments elsewhere, sympathies, little constitutions and rights of their own. (191-93)

Orlando is a fantasy where unity, and direction are given by two related themes, that no one is just one person and that time is not simply linear. In addition to "time on the clock" there are also both subjective or "mind" time and the cosmic or universal time. These themes are structural necessities making possible Orlando's fantastic transformations and longevity. Again, the theme of the individual-consciousness being a part of the group-consciousness is also elaborated. In *Orlando*, one consistent character is developed through the modifications caused by four hundred years of life. However, it may be said that *Orlando* was one of the light novels Virginia Woolf wrote to relax between the serious novels. But what Virginia Woolf gains with regard to spaciousness, she loses with regard to depth. Orlando becomes more or less a stage character and the environment as unreal and plain as canvas scenery. However, her contention that there is more similarity than difference between the sexes has been more effectively expounded in the form of a book in *A Room of One's Own.*

Orlando is wish-fulfilment, projecting an individual's thoughts and ideas. It appears unreal to others but is realistic to the individual concerned. It is purely a personal transaction between the mind and the pen of the author with no prior concern regarding the presentation for his readers. This mental process is accelerated because the individual finds that the life around him is unreal which does not really cater to his inner psychic needs.

It is from the psycho-dynamic principles of personality that response to external stimuli occurs. On interpreting the themes of fantasy, the mental framework of the author's mind may be evinced. It is through these expressions that we can interpret the individual's personality, symbolizing inner emotions and conflicts.

Fantasy literature is directly correlated to the mind and emotions of the author. Feelings are fantasized because they appear to be impossible proportions to the individual. These very different and apparently impossible dreams are the emotions of individuals, reaching out to symbols to express their inner meanings, their reality which is a combined projection of their consciousness and unconsciousness. Logic is replaced by pure emotions, irrational narratives are projected to counteract extreme rationalistic and intellectual norms of life. These soothing fairy-tale-like narratives give a lease of freshness and newness to the readers too. Those who respond attempt to identify their mental processes with that of the author and thus are released from intrapsychic pressure, of which they are consciously unaware. These intrapsychic pressures are the personal beliefs of the individual which are at variance with societal structure and patterns.

Fantasy expression takes root from certain personality-traits which have not been specifically analyzed and focussed upon by the individual himself. Framing these through processes on paper or verbalizing them moulds them into a story.

These flights of the mind may be scientifically oriented or be in deference to temporal barriers etc., depending on the state of mind and the fields of interest of the individual.

Social interaction is an interplay of social and personal demands requiring adjustments at every moment of our existence. If our lives do not cater to the required pattern, conflicts and turbulences result. External manifestation of these internal disturbances is brought about symbolically in various forms wherein the individual's personality is projected via the media of people and situations. These private evocations may at times be idiosyncratic but are a stepping-stone by which to conform to the social conventions.

In *The Analysis of Fantasy: Thematic Apperception-Technique in the Study of Personality,* William Henry writes.

> The Thematic Apperception-Technique is a device for the analysis of these underlining psychological needs, and feelings and the ways in which they are handled by the individual. Whether pathological or within the limits of normality, these underlying trends are manifested in terms of the ideas and symbols with which the individual communicates with others in ordinary non-test situations while somewhat unusual, the telling of stories to picture is not basically different from the tasks required of a person in regular social interaction. And,

similarly, the formulation of interrelated ideas in history form effect the pattern of ideas habitually utilized by the individual—full or constructed rich or impoverished, distorted or overly-cautious, reality-oriented or bizarre. The enthusiasms or hesitancies, the experimental gaps in awareness which give direction to the subjects ordinary action and conversation will similarly influence and direct his story telling.[28]

Fantasies are a manner of adaptation to outer realities in the unique manner of the individual.

NOTES

1. Vita Sackville-West, *The Heir* (London, Heinemann, 1922), p. 59.
2 David Daiches, *The Novel and the Modern World* (London: The University of Chicago Press, 1939), p. 185.
3. Avrom Fleishman, p. 139.
4. Virginia Woolf, *Orlando—A Biography* (London: The Hogarth Press, 1928), p. 108.
5. *Ibid.*
6. *A Writer's Diary*, 22nd October, 1927, p. 117.
7. *Ibid.*, p. 120.
8. Quentin Bell, *Virginia Woolf*, I, p. 138.
9. Henry Nicols, "The Psychology of Time," *American Journal of Psychology*, 3; from Robert E. Ornstein, *The Psychology of Consciousness* (New York, 1977), p. 100.
10. Gillian Beer, *Virginia Woolf and Pre-History*, from Eric Warner, *Virginia Woolf: A Centenary Perspective*, p. 121.
11. Roger Poole, *The Unknown Virginia Woolf* (London: Cambridge University Press, 1978), p. 51.
12. Stephen Spender, *World Within World* (London: Hamish Hamilton, 1951), p. 152.
13. Vita Sackville-West, "Virginia Woolf and Orlando," *The Listener*, Vol. 58, January 27, 1955, p. 158.
14. James Naremore, *The World Without a Self: Virginia Woolf and the Novel* (London: Yale University Press, 1973), p. 245.
15. Mircea Eliade, "Mephistopheles and the Androgyne or the Mystery

of the Whole," quoted from Avrom Fleishman, p. 146.

16. *The Waves* (London: The Hogarth Press, 1931), p. 199.
17. Herbert Marder, *Feminism and Art*, p. 105.
18. Catharine R. Stimpson, "Feminism and Feminist Criticism," *The Massachusetts Review*, Summer, 1983.
19. Caroline Heilbrun, *Towards a Recognition of Androgyny* (New York, A.A. Knopf, 1973), p. 123.
20. Maria Di Battista, p. 128.
21. Hermione Lee, p. 153.
22. Marcel Proust, *Remembrance of Things*, Part I, trans. C.K. Scott (London: Chatto and Windus, 1949), p. 15.
23. R.L.. Chambers, *The Novels of Virginia Woolf* (Edinburgh: Oliver and Boyd, 1947), p. 77.
24. *De Quincey's Works*, Vol. XIII, Edinburgh, 1890, p. 346. Quoted from N.C. Thakur, p. 91.
25. Elaine Showalter, p. 289.
26. Virginia Woolf, *Granite and Rainbow* (London: The Hogarth Press, 1958), p. 79.
27. Henri Bergson, *On Laughter in Comedy* (London: Macmillan, 1921), p. 73.
28. William E. Henry, *The Analysis of Fantasy: Thematic Apperception—Technique in the Study of Personality* (New York: John Urley and Sons, 1956), pp. 9-10.

The Semi-Transparent Envelope

After a brief sojourn in fantasy Virginia Woolf returns to her original theme of the individual-consciousness and group-consciousness which interact and complement each other in novels like *The Waves, The Years* and the posthumously-published *Between the Acts.*

The Waves is a beautiful prose-poem in which Virginia Woolf's talent reaches its zenith. The slumberous development of *The Moth* flowered into this ingenious series of soliloquies. In a diary-entry, we can evince a little of what was in her mind:

> Now is life very solid or very shifting? I am haunted by the two contradictions. This has gone on for ever; will last for ever; goes down on the bottom of the world—this moment I stand on. Also it is transitory, flying, diaphanous. I shall pass like a cloud on the waves. Perhaps it may be that though we change, one flying after another, so quick, so quick, yet we are somehow successive and continuous we human beings and show the light through.[1]

The title *The Waves* is encircled with an aura of mysticism, symbolizing the flux and continuity of life: the unfurling of six blooms, amidst eternity—life, time and the cosmic elements of the universe. It is composed of pure sense-impressions, portrayed in a realistic literary style, "with as little mixture of the alien and external as possible" as she expressed in *Modern Fiction:*

> The sun had not yet risen. . . . Gradually . . . as if the arm of a woman couched beneath the horizon had raised a lamp. . . higher and then higher until a broad flame became visible, an arc of fire burnt on the rim of the horizon and all round it the sea blazed gold.[2]

The Waves is a series of moments, with a diaphanous plot, delineating the progress of the individuals from their childhood to old age, from the rising to the setting of the sun, to "specify parallel moments as sunrise and birth, sunset and death."[3]

Virginia Woolf tries to depict that one moment inspires other innumerable moments very much like an atomic chain. This justifies the pattern of the novel which is a mass of moments presented over the years. "The pattern is supreme," writes E.M. Forster in his book on Virginia Woolf.[4]

Virginia Woolf voices her thoughts through Bernard:

> I begin to seek some design more in accordance with those moments of humiliation and triumph that come now and then undeniably. Lying in a ditch on a stormy day, when it has been raining, then enormous clouds come marching over the sky, tattered clouds, wisps of cloud. What delights me then is the confusion, the height, the indifference and the fury . . . and I forgotten, minute, in a ditch. Of story, of design, I do not see a trace then. (204-5)

The Waves is a beautiful theme portraying universality, a poem dealing with eternal truths which is a tough proposition. As the author herself explains: "I am not concerned with the single life but with lives together. I am trying to find in the folds of the past such fragments as time preserves . . . there was a napkin, a flower-pot and a book. I am telling the story of the world from the beginning and in a small room, whose windows are open."[5] The small room symbolizes the individual and the windows are the different facets of a personality, projected to the external world of time and space. The six characters portrayed are schematized in their worlds of consciousness, their external lives and activities being only a necessity for their physical survival.

Virginia Woolf stresses the psychological aspect and portrays the elusive moments of the consciousness because, unlike Henry James, she caters to our desire for visual transparencies. Henry James focusses only on the emotional depths of the individuals, ignoring the interaction with external life. David Daiches is of the opinion that *The Waves* is "at once . . . the most eloquent and least communicative of Virginia Woolf's novels."[6] Virginia Woolf utilizes a great deal of colour to project her evanescent ideas and the characteristics of her protagonists.

The technique cannot be pinpointed; but we can perceive that the novel and its soliloquies are a direct transcription of the consciousness of the author, very artistically portraying her complex and visionary ideas. It is an attempt to fuse poetry and realism in fiction. In the process of writing *The Waves,* Virginia Woolf voices her feelings:

> Suppose I could run all the scenes together more?—by rhythms chiefly. So as to avoid those cuts; so as to make the blood run like a torrent from end to end?[7]

From this diary-entry, we learn of the author's desire to unite all consciousnesses and make them one, like a blood-stream flowing in unison. Her inordinate experiment is logically construed, the technique of six individuals leading independent lives but diffused psychologically at a single point which is the author. It is an achievement to have captured flux in a form of stability, in a cadenced form, graduating in a series of physical and emotional developments in their relationships focussing with an intense realism on her narration.

The Waves is a simple progress of a day, with six children lying serenely at dawn and withered by age by dusk. As children awakened by the first sunbeams, their impressions are short and simple but typifying their personalities:

> "I see a ring" said Bernard, "hanging above me. It quivers and hangs in a loop of light."
>
> "I see a slab of pale yellow" said Susan, "spreading away until it meets a purple stripe."
>
> "I hear a sound," said Rhoda "cheep, chirp; cheep, chirp going up and down."
>
> "I see a globe," said Neville, "hanging down in a drop against the enormous flanks of some hill."
>
> " I see a crimson tassel," said Jinny, "twisted with gold threads."
>
> "I hear something stamping," said Louis, "A great beast's foot is chained. It stamps, and stamps, and stamps." (6-7)

These are the inarticulate expressions from which we must decipher the life of the inner consciousness of an individual. These innocent observations will be counteracted by the increased complexities of our personalities and society. Death and silence prevail in the closing chapters of their lives. This prose-poem portrays six individuals who have varied personalities: Bernard is a story-teller, communicative and easily accessible to society; Louis, a complex-ridden person, romanticist and rationalist; Neville, a poet and an introvert; Jinny is fascinated with her body and believes only in socializing; Susan desires motherhood, her own home and family; Rhoda, the silent one, finds no joy and sincerity in this world and finally takes her life. Percival is the only character who is never absorbed in their midst but is the fulcrum of their group. He is beautiful and assertive but finally meets with death falling from a horse far away in India.

They part after a time, the boys and girls go to different schools. The six friends are shown experiencing life at different levels and spheres of existence. Then they all meet at a dinner party to bid farewell to Percival who was going to India. Death plays a very important part in this novel as it does in other novels of Virginia Woolf.

In the next section, we are confronted with the news of Percival's death and the reaction of the six friends at this piece of tragic news. Meanwhile, they had all slid into their roles to be enacted in society. Bernard gets married but the birth of his son coincides with the death of Percival. Susan is blissfully married, having a farm and children. Jinny flits about in society, and Neville is still an emotionally disturbed individual, subconsciously pining for Percival. Louis is a successful businessman. Rhoda is a lonely individual travelling extensively to find peace, for which she even discontinues her relationship with Louis.

Rhoda condemned humanity as did Louis, but Rhoda submits to her anguish and Louis survives. They meet again in the next chapter but Percival is missing. Bernard gives us a running-commentary in the final chapter, a soliloquy which unfolds all the six individuals becoming one with him which he reflects in peace and solitude:

> Let me now raise my song of glory. Heaven be praised for solitude. Let me be alone. Let me cast and throw away this veil of being, this cloud that changes with the least breath, night and day, and all night and all day. While I sat here I have been changing. I have watched the sky change. I have seen clouds cover the stars, then free the stars, then cover the stars again. Now I look at their changing no more. Now no one sees me and I change no more. Heaven be praised for solitude that has removed the pressure of the eye, the solicitation of the body, and all need of lies and phrases. (253-54)

Virginia Woolf's state of mental health was in a precarious condition because of the four deaths which had taken place in her own home, "I am thinking of the stupid damage that their deaths inflicted."[5] She faced mental breakdown in 1895 and 1904 when her parents died. It was her brother Thoby's death which she projects in *Jacob's Room* and *The Waves*. She commemorates his memory as Percival which in French means the piercing of a veil. She records personal dilemma in her diary:

> Here in the few minutes that remain, I must record, heaven be

praised, the end of *The Waves*. I wrote the words O Death fifteen minutes ago, having reeled across the last ten pages with some moments of such intensity and intoxication that I seemed to only stumble after my own voice, or almost, after some sort of speaker (as when I was mad) I was almost afraid, remembering the voices that used to fly ahead. Anyhow, it is done; and I have been sitting these fifteen minutes in a state of glory, and calm, and some tears, thinking of Thoby and if I could write Julian Thoby Stephen 1881-1906 on the first page. I suppose not.[9]

Virginia Woolf's language in this novel is a flowing, rhythmic, colourful and realistic style. The author's desire is to project the inner psychological complexities which are imperceptible to us. Thus the detailed descriptions of even trivialities are of utmost importance as they depict the nuances and other characteristics of the little things in life. Third-person narrative characterizes the italicized passages. The soliloquies are naturally in the first-person narrative. Autobiographical details prevail all over the narrative. The soliloquies flow like a river, literally projecting the stream-of-consciousness technique. The language is passive, with no vehemence, and the narrative is serene. Metaphor is an important aspect in highlighting the external features of the world. The waves depict the cyclical stages of our lives, from the moment of its inception to its breaking on the shore; or the natural process of dawn to dusk forming a global whole.

In *The Waves*, Virginia Woolf makes an attempt to rent the veil of unreality asunder, with the perfect usage of language. She envelops nature itself with the utilization of italicized passages. Her language unfolds fleeting moments and projects them confidently and with equanimity. Emotionally sensitive characters desire silence and solitude which she signified with appropriate language exhibiting the inner consciousness of the characters.

Harold Nicolson says in a review:

As the symbol of her theme, Mrs. Woolf has taken the flux and

> reflux, the strange purposelessness of the sea as viewed from above and at a distance. Continually does this symbol cut across her vision, intruding into her images with its battering restlessness, its unplumbed mobility and its incessant renewals of shape and energy. Her whole intention is to depict the fluidity of human experience, the insistent interest of the inconsequent, the half-realised, the half-articulate, the unfinished and the unfinishable. She succeeds triumphantly. Her book sparkles with a thousand diamonds and at times it is shrouded with solemn cloud-reflection.[10]

A snail depicts the characteristics of an individual, an inner being and an outer shell to survive in society: "They spied a snail and tapped the shell against a stone. They tapped furiously methodically, until the shell broke and something slimy oozed from the crack." (93) Later Bernard says, "A shell forms upon the soft soul . . . shiny, upon which sensations, tap their beaks in vain." (219)

Virginia Woolf utilized the symbols of the waves and sea to depict life and reality. The mutability of life was impressed upon her by the frequent deaths in her home. N.C. Thakur has presented similarities in the usage of sea as the symbol of an individual self by T.S. Eliot in *The Dry Salvages*. He therefore writes, "The river is within us, the sea is all about us." It is interesting to note that Lord Buddha also employed the sea as a symbol of the Vast Unknown.[11]

Veils are an important symbol in the novel. The veiled description of sunrise to a veiled flow of water over the sands is the beginning of *The Waves*. Women were bound by tradition to be veiled in religious institutions. Maria Di Battista mentions this Pauline Veil which St. Paul had ordained. Virginia Woolf attacked the subjugation of women, even religion-based norms.[12] The omniscient narrator also can be referred to as 'veiled' because of her anonymity as we see in Henry James and Jane Austen; Virginia Woolf has very symbolically named her protagonist Percival which means to "rent the veil." There are innumerable references to the veil in this novel:

I will let the Russian Empress's veil flow about my shoulders. (46)

London is now veiled, now vanished, now crumbled, now fallen. (46)

. . . dusky veil was falling upon our endeavours. (239)

Let me cast and throw away this devil of being, this cloud that changes with the least breath. (253)

Life and death are juxtaposed in the novel, symbolized in the swinging door that Rhoda and Neville so often mention. The antitheses like morning and night, belief and atheism, reality and unreality are the extremes of life.

In 1928, Virginia Woolf made a diary-entry regarding her projection of time:

> What I want now to do is to saturate every atom. I mean to eliminate all waste, deadness, superfluity; to give the moment whole: whatever it includes. Say that the moment is a combination of thought; sensation, the voice of the sea. Waste, deadness, come from the inclusion of things that don't belong to the moment; this appalling narrative business of the realist: getting on from lunch to dinner: it is false, unreal, merely conventional. Why admit anything to literature that is not poetry—by which I mean saturated?[11]

Virginia Woolf develops a completely different aspect of temporal technique from her former novels. In *Mrs. Dalloway,* the duration of the novel was a single day. *Orlando* was framed in a period of four centuries. In *To the Lighthouse,* action took place in two days, with an intervening gap of ten years. *The Waves* was portrayed within the circumference of dawn to dusk, delineating the six individuals from their childhood to maturity. The author in reality was attempting to narrate timelessness with the continuous flux of the sea and waves. Even definite mention of time does not signify linear time or the inner working of the conscious. Spatial references, like London Hampton Court, Spain and Rome are made as they are essential for the physical existence of the individuals.

The author is imbued with the joy of a single moment of revelation. The physical existence of the individuals diffuses with the temporal factor wherein only sense impressions are conspicuous. It was eternity, the eternal moment which Virginia Woolf desired to focus upon. Memory is an important aspect in the transience of time; but consciousness is forever changing. As Bergson states, "Consciousness cannot go through the same state twice"[14] Virginia Woolf's tunnelling process unites the past to the present by recollection and evocation of feelings. Memory is not static and with experience our views and conceptions of life too change and these are linked to the present.

Virginia Woolf built up her characters with the technique of repetition, with threads of continuity integrating the story with different leitmotifs.

Louis is the son of a banker in Brisbane and his own Australian accent disgusts him. He is an intelligent boy but envies the athletes. He is thus filled with complexes and persistently hears the stamping of a chained beast and the thudding of the waves, "my roots are threaded, like fibres in a flower-pot, round and round about the world. I do not wish to come to the top and live in the light of this great clock, yellow-faced, which ticks and ticks." (16) The weight of the world is on his shoulders. Even though he is successful in his business, loneliness and depression overcome him. It is only in solitude that he gets his bearings: "I shall assemble a few words and forge round us a hammered ring of beaten steel." (144)

Percival is placed on a higher level of existence. He understands Shakespeare and Catullus more than the others and is a sportsman. He is the novel's imperceptible and unfathomable centre and an idealized hero:

> "Let us hold it for one moment," said Jinny; "love hatred, by whatever name we call it, this globe whose walls are made of Percival, of youth and beauty, and something so deep sunk within us that we shall perhaps never make this moment out of one man again." (124)

We know him through the consciousness of others, and it is their common love which creates an atmosphere of communion. He is the idealized hero of six individuals whose early death is tragic. But they absorb him in their beings, never to be parted from him.

The most important of the six characters is Bernard who is a novelist:

> Bernard, in public, bubbles; in private, is secretive. . . . I have to effect different transitions; have to cover the entrances and exits of several different men who alternately act their parts as Bernard. . . . I also am too complex. In my case something remains floating, unattached. (64-65)

Bernard crystallizes his personality and identifies himself with Byron, Shelley and Hamlet though he also establishes himself as one with his five friends:

> I am not one person: I am many people; I do not altogether know who I am—Jinny, Susan, Neville, Rhoda or Louis; or how to distinguish my life from theirs. (237)

At times he feels that he is without a self and that his world is sunless and weightless. But the phrase-maker restores joy to his life: "I wish, then, after this somnolence to sparkle, many-faceted under the light of my friend's faces. I have been traversing the sunless territory of non-identity." (9) Marriage to Bernard is the death of his self since he has to traverse a margin of unknown territory. He survives the shock of the corruption of life and he achieves unity between the two worlds of consciousness. Bernard is reminiscent of Camus's hero Sisyphus:

> who is as much through his passions as through his torture . . his hatred for death, and his passion for life won him that unspeakable penalty in which the whole being is exerted towards accomplishing nothing.[15]

The last sentence of the novel—"The waves broke on the shore" (256)—is Bernard's complete identification of his consciousness, both mythical and empirical, with the universe while he is able to overcome his past sensations of loneliness and non-identity.

Susan resembles Mrs. Ramsay in her desire for a family life:

> The only sayings I understand are cries of love, hate, rage and pain. . . . I shall never have anything but natural happiness. It will almost content me. I shall go to bed tired. I shall lie like a field bearing crops in rotation; . . . I shall be lifted higher than any of you on the backs of the seasons. . . . I shall be debased and hide-bound by the bestial and beautiful passion of maternity. (113)

She is of a gentle, tender nature as her observation of a pale yellow slab of light indicates. She dislikes the rigidity of schedules and loses her identity amidst the fertility rites of her home: "I want to give, to be given, and solitude in which to unfold my possessions." (45)

Neville on the other hand experiences the turbulence of inexpressible poetry and the pangs of unrequited love. He also suffers from a sense of loss of identity and negative complexes like "Whether I am doomed always to cause repulsion in those I love." (128) Insecurity undermines his confidence and his homosexual tendency increases his morbidity which triggers off a guilt-ridden personality. Percival's death is like a punishment for him. In reality he desires an emotional relationship on an intellectual plane. It is significant to note that St. John Hirst, William Dodge and Neville are all intellectuals with homosexual tendencies.

Neville's extreme sensitivity is projected by the death among the apple trees. The dead man and the apple trees get diffused in his consciousness. We perceive his final conversion to heterosexuality from his soliloquies.

Rhoda is of a fragile and sensitive nature. She can never identify herself with the world: a sense of unreality envelops her;

thus, she finds consciousness of her own being intolerable:

> I am thrust back to stand burning in this clumsy, this ill-fitting body, to receive the shafts of his indifference and his scorn, I who long for marble columns and pools on the other side of the world where a swallow dips her wings. (128)

She stabilized her existence by touching a solid object or identifying herself with Jinny and Susan. Her sense of unsubstantiality places her outside the realm of time:

> I am not yet twenty-one. I am to be broken. I am to be derided all my life. I am to be cast up and down among these men and women, with their twitching faces, with their lying tongues, like a cork on a rough sea. Like a ribbon of weed I am flung far every time the door opens. I am the foam that sweeps and fills the uttermost rims with whiteness; I am also a girl, here in this room.[16]

She exists on the rim, the outer crust of society. Septimus Smith too, like Rhoda, suffered from manic depression, and committed suicide—a final union with nature and solitude. McLaurin writes:

> A poet who is concerned with absence would obviously interest a writer who wishes to write a novel about silence and whose characters so often see an emptiness at the heart of life. *The Waves* is in many ways a symbolist novel, and in the figure of Rhoda, Virginia Woolf embodies the area of ambiguity between 'purity' and 'sterility' which is one of Mallarme's principal concerns.[17]

Jinny is a socialite, imbued with the world of paint and sensuality. She is flighty by nature and a hedonist. She possesses a defiant attitude and experiences the torments of daily living. Apparently, she harbours an intense fascination for the opposite sex. But tragically, she fails to establish a lasting relationship with any of them. It is by the extreme sensitivity of her body-rhythm that she bypasses reality. It is with grace and equanimity that she feels a oneness with the ceaseless rhythms of the sea: "Lifts rise and fall; trains stop, trains start as regularly as the waves of the sea." (214)

Every individual in the novel is a unit by himself and is also a composite part of life as a whole. The Individual sprouts from one's individual consciousness and unconsciousness, choices in life, his values and grades of emotions and experiences. Neville suffers from a loss of identity and in order to develop it he goes to Bernard. But Bernard instantly recoils from him because he disapproves of his untidiness and envies his remorseless intellect by inventing humorous stories. Bernard's type of intellect focuses on his many-faceted beings—one of them being his desire for identification with the literary figures:

> The tree alone resisted our eternal flux. For I changed and changed; was Hamlet, was Shelley, was the hero, whose name I now forget, of a novel by Dostoevsky; was for a whole term, incredibly, Napolean; but was Byron chiefly. (214)

This passage is a partial exposition of two personalities. Distinctions can only be made in this manner, by little habitual acts—Bernard's trusting of little boys, Rhoda's dreams of swallows and pillars, Susan's screwed-up pocket handkerchief, Neville's call to a certain individual and Jinny's yellow scarf.

The chained beast projects Louis's sense of insecurity. Rhoda too portrays a similar complex when she sees the bird singing alone and the snail flattened on the grass. Occasionally, we evince a strain of sexual desire in her, by which she escapes for a while from the fangs of depression. Jinny exists amidst sex, paint and men. They are the fount of her energy, the reason for her to live. Neville is a homosexual which is his line of existence. Sex does not provide any sense of security to either of them in their later lives. Solitude is the only answer to excessive socializing. Virginia Woolf wrote in her diary:

> I am going to face certain things. It is going to be a time of adventure and attack rather lonely and painful I think. But solitude will be good for a new book.[18]

Silence intervenes the series of soliloquies which reveal the working of the consciousness of each individual protecting his individuality in a dialectic manner. Certain monologues reflect the characteristics of others and thus we know them intimately, even without normal exchanges of conversation. The individuals not wholly integrated, physically or emotionally, with society. Silence and soliloquies are their ideal form of interaction in the world of their consciousness. They do exist in society but only for survival in a routine manner, like the rise and fall of a wave. Unlike *The Voyage Out* and *Night and Day*, physical descriptions are more or less eliminated, the schemata being concentrated in the inner world of the selves. As a result we can even strike up relationships with the character on our plane of consciousness. This is possible due to the uninhibited description of their consciousness. Silence too speaks volumes and Virginia Woolf has succeeded in writing a novel on silence, as predicted by Hewet. It is in silence and solitude that characters like Bernard, Neville and Rhoda gain fortitude to face experiences of daily existence. We can visualize emotions in the purest form, with the author's visionary and intuitive powers ascending heights of supremacy. This is what is meant by living, Virginia Woolf seems to say, this continual awareness, this ruthless clinging to the truth of thoughts, sensations and emotions. The rest is superficial; the web Virginia Woolf weaves is full of colours and sounds and scents and it is no barren abstract analysis of a life. It lives and moves. And behind it all we sense the colour, "the white radiance of eternity, the presence of Reality itself."[19]

Reality and society are on opposite planes. Truth can be envisioned in solitude only and in rare instances, people do experience a visionary moment, a contact with reality when in company. Rhoda prefers solitude and nature where she can be more at ease than in company. She is never attracted by an intellectual life. Music fulfills her aesthetic sensibility and it is through this that she expresses her philosophy of life, which is connected to truth and beauty. Rhoda's final illumination, the momentary realism which engulfs her, is Percival's death. "The lightning has gashed," is similar to Clarissa's reaction on hearing the news of Septimus's death. But Rhoda's sensitive nature creates a feeling of unreality in her and, unlike Clarissa, she cannot identify herself with people: "who communes with her own consciousness and socializes on an equal footing. Rhoda feels that I am alone in a hostile world, the human face is hideous." (136) Winifred Holtby has aptly termed the individual's consciousness as a "submarine cave," depicting unconscious play of thoughts and feelings where reason and logic have no place.[20]

The schematization of the characters of the novel is dialectically similar to the movement of the waves. The characters are initially encapsulated in a single space and later they are portrayed in their individual paths of life when they converge to a point. Death will finally disintegrate this union, like the waves breaking on the shore. Memory is the integrating factor, like a thread weaving through their consciousness. A single individual exhibits varied consciousness, like Clarissa Dalloway who identifies her subterranean being with that of Septimus and Orlando projects various personalities in a single life-time. In *The Waves*, the separate destinies of the characters decide their individual fates but their love for Percival unites them all:

> We are drawn into this communion by some deep, some common emotion. Shall we call it, conveniently, "love?" Shall we say "love of Percival" because Percival is going to India. No, that is too small, too particular a name. We cannot attach the width and spread of our feelings to so small a mark. (118)

They are drawn into a circle of love and they feel illuminated when a sense of joy pervades them which is experienced in the interlude of silence between each monologue. They react to Percival's death in solitude where the relationships between Rhoda, Louis, Neville, Jinny and Bernard will finally dissolve. The moments of communion are preserved in the sacred terrain of their soul and their private visions unite them together. They approach each other with varying entities and personalities and are enjoined at least in certain spheres of time and space, a common belief—like the scene of the willow tree depicting reality and the apple-tree projecting death, "the tree alone resisted our eternal flux." (248) What each one was as a child is manifested in their consciousness and this governs their final attitude in life. Louis, Bernard, Susan and Jinny and Neville tried to compromise with life, either in the solitude of their own company or in the social milieu they had settled in. Rhoda was threatened with a feeling of non-identity. She is portrayed in an extreme version of tension between socializing and isolation, which is a recurring motif in all the novels of Virginia Woolf. Even Louis who tried to live with an authoritative and powerful social life could never outgrow his inherent inferiority complex and was overcome with a secret loneliness. But, unlike Rhoda, he survives in society. Bernard is the self-realized character who manages to unite with the mystical world and is ready to welcome death after overcoming his unrealistic feeling and his question of "Who am I?" (248) Finally, he sums up the meaning of his life. Innumerable realizations have dawned on him with the passage of time. One of them being that the apparently beautiful designs and patterns of life are false and that each individual was born with a different personality. Louis hated physical contact but Jinny thrived on physical interaction desiring an infinitismal amount of love; Rhoda could not bear torture and cruelty but Susan was tough, earthy and practical by nature. Neville was artistic and orderly and Bernard, while preserving his separate identity, fuses himself with all of them. He is able to serenely contemplate the personality of a complete human being, leading him to a direct perception into the whirlpool of life which is at the very core of existence, thus evincing truth and beauty with an equally artistic language which communicates the true state of an individual's mind:

> Having sifted the elements of a human-life sensation, the subconscious, self-consciousness, sex, guilt, among others—the chief soliloquist undertakes a sustained enquiry into the nature of selfhood. It is Bernard's achievement to gain in theoretical clarity while realizing himself in practice; just as his life is a steady growth in imaginative and expressive power, so his sense of self develops through a number of alternative theories to a final statement (which we can identify with the author's own). This parallel process is one of the finest achievements of *The Waves* design and affords some of Woolf's views of the individual's relation to death, art, and the universe.[21]

Death sublimates all differences. In life we can renew our creative energies and diversify our lifestyles but death is the levelling factor. For Bernard, the artist's identity merges in the flux of ordinary life and "the fin" does not rise any more:

> And in me too the wave rises. It swells; it arches its back. I am aware once more of a new desire, something rising beneath me like the proud horse whose rider first spurs and then pulls him back. What enemy do we now perceive advancing against us, you whom I ride now, as we stand pawing this stretch of pavement? It is death. Death is the enemy. It is death against whom I ride with my spear couched and my hair flying back like a young man's, like Percival's, when he galloped in India. I strike spurs into my horse. Against you I will fling myself, unvanquished and unyielding, O Death! (255-56)

Virginia Woolf's philosophy of life is that power and wealth do not bring fulfilment and that the emptiness in the precincts of the heart remains if it is not replenished by an awareness of the artist's perception of life and death.

II

The Years follows the *The Waves* after an interval of six years and this is also dominated by the conception of time, which is the central theme of the novel. A flood of memories and emotions flow through *The Years* with the individual generations patterned into various motifs in the fabric. With the passage of time, changes are wrought, birth and decay set in automatically, and thus the years enact the role of protagonists, integrating or disintegrating. This novel is directly related to *Orlando* and *Between the Acts.* The plot is nothing but the enumeration of a series of incidents regarding the Pargiter family. Virginia Woolf's involvement was not with the desultory and routine affairs of life but her interest lay in focussing on the sense-impressions, with the projection of fragmentary and discontinuous conversations and thought-processes. A direct transcription of thoughts presented not in a short and staccato style but beautifully woven and assimilated into the narrative. Howard Spring in his review of *The Years* writes:

> We seem to subsist in this book not on the bright surface of time, with its sallies and bubbles, its bickering round rocks that look immense but never stay the flow, but in the apparently still yet irresistible undercurrent of things that lie too deep for tears.[22]

In his novel, we experience the author's boundless vision and extraordinary power of perception which fluctuates pendulum-like between the past and the present. Generations are portrayed parallel to the simultaneity of life, as in Tolstoy's *War and Peace* and Galsworthy's *Forsyte Saga.*

Memory is an essential device utilized by Virginia Woolf to impress her ideas and feelings upon the reader. The simple sound of hammering at Oxford makes a deep impression on Kitty which persists when she is married. Wagner Siegfried's leitmotif was the sound of hammering which she attended with Edward. McLaurin notes that even in *Time Regained,* Marcel's memory is triggered by the sound of hammering.[23] Eleanor too relives the past in the present moment:

> My life's been other people's lives, Eleanor thought—my father's; Morris's; my friend's lives; Nicholas's Fragments of a conversation with him came back to her. Either I'd been lunching with him or dining with him, she thought. It was in a restaurant. There was a parrot with a pink feather in a cage on the counter. . . .
>
> Just as I was thinking of you! she repeated. Indeed it was like a part of her, a sunk part of her, coming to the surface.[24]

Virginia Woolf's masterful technique of registering impressions is unique. Eleanor's initial shock at the news of Parnell's death is presented graphically and meticulously from the subconscious to the conscious level, pegging her thoughts to the surrounding environment. She wanted to project "the dimensions of the human beings,"[25] by breaking away completely from her initial technique and form of narrative. She was in search of an even more concise form, for an even closer integration of the psyche and physique. As she wrote in her diary, "New combination in psychology and body. . . . This will be the next novel, after *The Years*."[26]

The failure of a vision results from the fragmentation of an individual's thoughts and this may be due to the lack of words. Thus her language varies in tone from situation to situation. A mere repetition of words is sometimes attempted to impress a thought upon the reader; although it might produce a jarring effect. In the last chapter there is a repetition of the word "spoons" where it might be interpreted as a symbol of the littleness of life when compared to the ultimate where it can very well be described as a measuring of life with "coffee spoons."

The routine life of the individual members of the Pargiter family was chronicled within a timespan of fifty years, from 1880 to 1930. Virginia Woolf noted in her diary:

> the exalted sense of being above time and death which comes

from being again in a writing mood. And this is not an illusion, so far as I can tell.[27]

The rebirth of experience in the final chapter, after years of submerged existence, should expand and deepen the present. The last chapter is a single evening, forming a sonorous vault that echoes and reechoes the past. This chapter can be compared to *Time Remembered* which is the final book of Marcel Proust's *Remembrance of Things Past.* The last chapter is dotted with a persistent awareness of both inner and outer device, especially the latter, with the innumerable references to the striking of various clocks all over London. Kitty Lasswade, like Orlando, was the only character who escaped to the countryside to gain peace and serenity and for a short space of time to revel in solitude.

The Years is a fictional saga commencing from the Victorian era to the present generation. In the process, Virginia Woolf has portrayed the minds of the protagonists in a psycho-analytical manner. The Pargiters lived in Abercorn Terrace and the inamtes were Mr. and Mrs. Pargiter and their seven children: Eleanor, Edward, Morris, Delia, Milly, Martin and Rose. The Colonel had a brother Digby, his wife Eugenie and their daughters Maggie and Sally. Eventually Mrs. Pargiter dies and the children grow up. Their lives are portrayed along with their physical and emotional realities. Eleanor joins a philanthropic organization and sacrifices her youth in order to care for the family, especially her father. Delia supports the Irish revolutionaries; Rose gets involved with the Suffragette Movement; Edward gets interested in intellectual life as an University don; Martin settles down as a retired colonel; Morris becomes a successful lawyer; Milly becomes a housewife. Kitty Malone was Eleanor's maternal cousin who married Lord Lasswade. Maggie was happily married to Rene, a Frenchman. Sara loved Nicholas who was unfortunately a homosexual. Morris's children Peggy and North were displeased with the norms of the present times. The novel ends on an optimistic and interesting note. There are thought-provoking discussions juxtaposed between members of different generations. Virginia Woolf's life is reflected all through the narrative. Kitty's fascination for her History teacher Lucy Craddock is similar to the author's admiration for Janet Case, her Greek teacher, "and how great a visionary part she has played in my life, till the visionary became a part of the fictions, not of the real life."[28] Janet's case was represented by Virginia Woolf as her alter-ego because she was powerless in face of certain social discrepancies wherein a woman was debarred from exhibiting her emotions. Being an individual of extreme sensitivity, she learnt to disconnect her own private feelings and created an alter-ego, Miss Jan, in an attempt to silence her own voice. Louise Desalvo writes:

> But not entirely, for throughout this diary, throughout this entire look at the coming into womanhood of one of this century's most gifted writers, Woolf maintains, through the persona of Miss Jan, a private self whom she allows to express her feelings. It is an unfortunate necessity, but an accommodation, none the less, to the way women are socialized to silence their own voices. This diary also records how a young woman, even as she concedes to society's insistence that she develop in this way, manages to keep a small part of herself for herself, a fictionalized self, a 'Miss Jan' whom she will lock up within the covers of a brown gilt diary even as she is forced to lock up her feelings and wishes and desires.[29]

Virginia Woolf had mastered the ultimate in literary creation, that of successfully integrating thought and matter into the innumerable dimensions of human beings.

The Years is an autobiographical novel projecting Virginia Woolf's ideas in a social background. Nicholas Pomjalovsky was a portrayal of Lytton Strachey whose engagement to Virginia Woolf was broken due to his homosexual tendencies. Rose's encounter with a sordid man exhibiting himself is the author's personal experience in her youth which Leonard Woolf had recorded in his autobiography.

To Virginia Woolf, coins were symbolic of female emancipation, resulting from economic freedom after generations of servitude to the patriarchy. This is the central symbol in this novel shouldering the destiny of women, promising liberty and a comfortable, serene existence. She imagines a man's pocket as a bottomless pit overflowing with silver and portrays a woman with only a few coins clenched in her hand:

> Millions of things came back to her. Atoms danced apart and massed themselves. But how did they compose what people called a life? She clenched her hands and felt the hard little coins she was holding. Perhaps there's "I" at the middle of it; she thought; a knot; a centre; and again she saw herself sitting at her table drawing on the blotting paper, digging little holes from which spokes radiated. (280)

This dot symbolizes Eleanor's mental illumination; her realization of truth and reality; the centrality of life. As Marder puts it, it is "Eleanor's mystical liberation, her discovery of the core of the self."[30]

Besides the coin, wind and smoke are also prominent symbols in this novel, depicting vast open space in which the wind billows and warps the smoke with freedom. The hollowness and meaninglessness of life is symbolized by life's grotesqueness and is projected by images like the eczema behind the ears of Mira's dog; the noseless violet seller, the pock-marked face of the exhibitionist; Colonel Pargiter's deformed hand resembling the claws of a bird; Sara, a deformed girl, appears like a dishevelled fowl, standing outside St. Paul's.

Eleanor is the main character in the novel and she is introduced as a twenty-two year old girl involved in managing the home because of her mother's ill-health. In 1891, she had sacrificed Whatney's love and abandoned her personal freedom to take care of her father; thus bending to the patriarchal yoke and forsaking life's joys and pleasures. Later, on meeting Nicholas who suited her standard of an ideal husband, her desire for marriage was momentarily evoked. Much of her thinking is governed by her response to Nicholas's idealistic goal of human reformation: "We cannot make laws and religion to fit because we do not know ourselves." (245)

Eleanor often felt a sense of having experienced the present moment in the past—déja vu, the present moment being connected with invisible threads to the past. Time can mould any individual and Eleanor achieves a whole personality with the passage of time. This is similar to the experience of Orlando when Eleanor discovers that with the advancement of science in time, life has been changed because of gadgets like aeroplanes, telephones, electricity and automobiles. She envisions a gigantic pattern in the process in the personalities of Peggy and North. Even at seventy, she is able to contemplate life. Her experience helps her indulge in philosophizing about life, "'But I meant this world!' she said. 'I meant, happy in this world—happy with living people.'" (295) Eleanor attempts to recreate her vision of life within the space of her cupped hand. She is the only character who shines like the consistent rays of a lighthouse and diffuses with life as Mrs. Ramsay's being diffuses with the third beam of the lighthouse. Eleanor's sense of perception penetrates the surface-hardness of life and she is engulfed in her vision of reality. Like Lily Briscoe, she identifies herself with the ordinary aspects of life.

Delia's watchwords due to her passionate involvement with Parnell, an Irish Revolutionary, were Freedom and Justice. Delia impatiently awaited her ailing mother's death. This would do away with all her tense moments and give them relief and freedom. She is quietly thrilled when her end comes but is disgusted at her father's shameful pretence of sorrow. In due course Delia gets married and finds emotional security in her home, with her husband and their three children. She had dispensed away with all bindings and rigidity of tradition, riding triumphantly on the crest of the wave of existence, sweeping Eleanor alone with her exuberance.

Rose too was a firebrand suffragettist and has been jailed for stone-throwing. Kitty Malone was the daughter of an Oxford don. Like Katharine Hilbery, she had to cater to her mother's desires and lead an obsolete, frivolous and inane life of socializing. She fulfilled her desire for an earthy, down-to-earth life in her friend Nell Robson's house, in its crude atmosphere of hencoops, stained tableware and noisy hammering. Like Clarissa Dalloway, she married a dignitary and her lifestyle was transformed. But even this ornate life as Lady Lasswade irked her at times, "I always want to take a knife and scrape it all off." (103)

The more pathetic individual in the novel is Sara who is portrayed as a deformed girl and is forced to accept life with an sense of resignation. As she had to adjust in a cruel and relentless society, she even as a child identified herself with the story of Antigone. The masculine sex figured in her thoughts as cruel and demanding and she had a morbid obsession with death. Sara's destiny and her psychological attitude are portrayed very beautifully. Her lazy manners are only a pretension to save herself from being exposed to an unsympathetic society protecting her unsatiated desires and her extreme sensitivity. Even the man she loves is beyond her reach since he is a homosexual. This fact too, she accepts with extreme refinement and courage, repressing her feelings with grace and equanimity: "She became something; a root; lying sunk in the earth; veins seemed to thread the cold mass." (103)

Peggy was Eleanor's niece and a doctor by profession. She was enamoured of the past and the past memories of Eleanor gave her peace and a feeling of security. She desired complete freedom of mind and body. Virginia Woolf was projecting G.E. Moore's philosophy of "a state of mind" wherein Peggy wanted to experience reality where there would be "real laughter, real happiness, and this fractured world was whole, whole and free." (297) She had lost her brother Charles in the war and the bitterness persisted in her heart. She became a sceptic, doubting one and all, even her brother North.

North had just returned from Africa, still in a phase of adjustment with London and society. He watched people with amusement, considering them as bubbles in the stream of life. He noticed a few strands of grey hair in his sister's hair and realized that they were aging and were not so very young. He was aware of the passing generations and his thought congealed in a verse from Catallus: "Suns may rise and set; we, when our short day has closed, must sleep on in one perpetual night."[38] Death was the ultimate state of being towards which each one of us is heading. But life, has to be lived before we attain this permanent state. A glass of champagne reverts his mind to brighter trends of thought, about life and its renewal. Thomas Wolfe's philosophy of life is like the isolated bubbles traversing in any fluid. Man is doomed to perpetual isolation—this is the central theme of his works. Virginia Woolf too believes in this theory. Silence and solitude are leitmotifs which are inbuilt in all her narratives. As North, walking on the road, wonders: "Was solitude good; was society bad?" (237)

Primitive men always lived in groups, more for the need to survive than for the desire for company. With the growing independence of man, social awareness is on the decline. The introduction of innovatory modes of existence is projected in characters like Sara and Nicholas. Virginia Woolf was able to cater simultaneously to both the modern trends and traditional norms of existence. The traditional form was characterized in the marriage of Milly and Hugh Gibbs. Thirty years of playing the role of husband and wife had precipitated to chew-chew-chew and tut-tut-tut, resembling the half-inarticulate munchings of animals in their stalls. Milly also attempts to keep the family together: "She cast a net over them; she made them all feel one family; he had to think of their relation in common; but it was an unreal feeling." (285) North did not relish this gesture of Milly and thought it to be an artificial manner of existence. Individuality and the integration of an individual with society were Virginia Woolf's constant concerns and were projected via her characters. Like the guest Kitty Lasswade had in the Opera:

> He had forgotten her. He had forgotten himself. . . . There was an odd look on his face as if he were in two worlds at once and had to draw them together. (143)

Eleanor and Nicholas share immense compatibility in their friendship. Each had their loneliness to combat. Nicholas was a homosexual and, imbued within this curse, he dreamt of a New World: "'The soul—the whole being,' he explained. He hollowed his hands as if to enclose a circle. 'It wishes to expand, to adventure, to form new combinations.'" (226) Eleanor with her profound adjustment has attained a state of androgyny wherein she can perceive society on a broad perspective. She did identify her present life with an empty jug and falling leaves. This is one of the series of insights of extra-physical life, new ripples of consciousness which Eleanor experiences in Delia's party.

Virginia Woolf wanted to "keep the individual and the sense of things coming over and over again and yet changing. That's what's so difficult, to combine the two."[32] Peggy could only break a fragment of he vision and present it to North, causing sorrow because of misinterpretation of meaning. An inadequacy of social communion and solitude pervaded the final chapter of the novel. But the fragmentation of thoughts is presented in an attempt to portray the individual consciousness, the indivisible 'I': "What would the world be, he said to himself— ... without 'I' in it?" (185) Hermione Lee compares Virginia's involvement with the soul and the individual 'I' with that of Chekhov. Virginia Woolf in her essay *The Russian Point of View* mentions her affinity with Chekhov in the field of spiritual involvement as portrayed in their writings Hermione Lee writes:

> But the soul and society cannot be simply divided. The search for goodness necessitates the search for a modus vivendi with other people, not in solitude. The enemy to goodness, both in the Victorian home and in the public world, is the voice of egotism that says "I," "I," "I." Eleanor, Sara and Nicholas, Martin, Maggie and Renny, Martin, Morris and Peggy, all want to combat that enemy, but have no ready-made defences. Possibly the only alternative to the domineering "I" is "the world without a self."[33]

Renny was an ideal husband and led a truly peaceful life with Maggie. As for his profession, he admits, "I help them to make shells," and a mask had come down over his face. A man who made shells, a man who loved peace, a man of science, a man who cried."

(265) A perfectly androgynous person portraying an ideal state of being, for harmonious existence in society.

The visionary heroine is not an ethereal, extra-corporeal person, but an individual who lives among people, leading an ordinary life and adjusting equally with her own individual self and her social being. Eleanor is endowed with an integrated androgynous personality, as is Renny. As in *The Waves*, the identity of the characters is not completely dissolved; the protagonists retain their personalities with society. Even North Pargiter who prefers solitude attends parties and socializes. In her book, Hermione Lee advocates social interdependence, supporting her argument with voices of Coleridge, Rousseau, Whitman and George Sand. Quoting George Sand, she says:

> All existences are interdependent, and any human being who was to present his own in isolation, without linking it with that of his fellow creatures, would only be presenting a riddle in need of solving. His individual existence, by itself, has no significance or importance whatsoever. It only takes on some kind of meaning by becoming a fragment of life in general by merging with the individuality of all of us, and it is only by this means that it becomes a part of history.[34]

This novel does not mainly pursue either a necessity for the individual's social existence but professes that there is a need for both.

The caretaker's children symbolize the dawning of the new era. They commence with silence and a little later, burst out into song which sounds unintelligible to the older generation. But the Pargiter family unite with wonderful optimism under the awning of dawn, heralding the onset of a new day: "The sun had risen, and the sky above the houses wore an air of extraordinary beauty, simplicity and peace." (331) Avrom Fleishman writes: "The Present-Day stands with the 'Wandering Rocks' section of *Ulysses* as a grand attempt to synthesize a vision of life, from the various perspectives of a modern multitude."[35]

Virginia Woolf presented a vision of society camouflaged in humour, like a clown's motley apparel. Every individual is a constituent of society living in accordance to his personality. Society too is like a motley structure, like the picture which they all drew, "Each of them had drawn a different part of a picture." (297) Even amidst this extreme projection of the individual, a structure is always perceived. Similarly, even with our inherent personality-traits, we have to learn to adjust in society and live as a harmonious whole.

The novel ends on a symbolic note when Eleanor perceives a couple descending from a taxi. This is a triumph of Virginia Woolf's feministic ideals, her moment of joy and success. The post-generations are shown grouped in a very impressive manner, symbolized by a serene dawn ushering in the new generation represented by the solemn and silent children. This strikes a discordant note, especially their indecipherable language where harmony reigns supreme. Eleanor returns to the party in a mood of ecstasy with a hope of renewal, envisioning a better world. Like Mrs. Dalloway, she rejoins her guests in an enlightened state of mind—pervaded by a mood of extraordinary beauty, simplicity and peace.

III

It the waves's process of formation and disintegration is the leitmotif woven into the narrative of the novel, with the various eras forming a mosaic-like pattern in the fabric, *Between the Acts* refers to the intervening time gaps, in which we perceive the variegated personalities of the protagonists providing significant information:

> That the title of the novel is *Between the Acts* itself announces this ordering of priorities, time will be treated as an aesthetic occasion and the action of the drama to unfold will transpire in a self-insulated and self-enclosed aesthetic scene outside or apart from history's battle grounds.[36]

Between the Acts, the last novel of Virginia Woolf, was published posthumously and the narration covers a day at a country house, during which a historical pageant is performed. Miss La Trobe who organizes the show on a day in June in the year 1939 did so with the intention of conveying her theory, that the historical past is an inextricable part of the present consciousness which along with it forms a complete vision of life. *Between the Acts* follows the same pattern that has been elaborated in *Orlando* and *The Waves*. When the pageant is unrolled, the audience is able to witness Chaucerian, Elizabethan, Restoration, Victorian and Present-Day episodes, with strategic interludes, all within a specified time. Virginia Woolf's attempt was to capture the essence of British History and present-day reality. This is a plot that never really appealed to Virginia Woolf because experience and reality can never be portrayed in a planned manner.

Virginia Woolf's infinitely beautiful and inimitable novels can be classified under classicist literature. *Between the Acts* is a novel that adapts lyrical style—the historical pageant is presented mainly in verse. Since plot has no significant role in her novels, the fabric of the narration need not be woven with any particular design. Therefore, the texture of her novels is loose and flowing, moving leisurely like a stream of water.

Virginia Woolf could immerse herself in the murky sordidity of life, in the ambience of truth and reality and thus be simultaneously transfused in the ethereal beauty of mysticism. Hence her novels are condensed with all these influences resulting in novels with lyrical intensities. *Between the Acts* gave Virginia Woolf real joy as she has recorded in her diary, feeling "a little triumphant" and thinking it "an interesting attempt in a new method . . . more quintessential than the others."[37]

Woolf has adopted the mirroring process which has reflected the translucent emotions and consciousness of the characters along with the surrounding landscape, as is seen in the incident where Mrs. Giles Oliver gazes into the three-fold mirror so that she could visualize three separate versions of her face. (14) This multi-dimensional technique is an effective device utilized in psychological novels. This novel overtly projects a vacuous and bleak picture with nothing constructive to peg our thoughts upon but the quintessence of the narrative is thought-provoking and appeals to the sensibility of the reader. The ideas are presented in a dialectical manner, projecting drama on the stage and the activities of a few characters between the acts in a comprehensive manner—one being purely dramatic, and the other focussing on the inner beings while encompassing a mature vision of life and reality. Another effective technique that Woolf utilizes is the juxtaposition of the mundane and the prosaic with the ethereal and poetic, like the soliloquy of Isa:

> The words made two rings, perfect rings, that floated them . . . like two swans down stream. But his snow-white breast was circled with a tangle of dirty duckweed; and she too, in her webbed feet was entangled, by her husband, the stockbroker. (8)

Virginia Woolf's mastery over language, combined with her poetic sensibility, was a rare quality. As Edwin Muir comments: "She has never written better prose than the prose in this last book."[38] Woolf's use of the language is moulded into a lyrical style by her aesthetic love for melody and beauty.

Virginia Woolf has been able to project the whole of English History in a short space of time, with the help of a handful of actors. The past and the present are juxtaposed with the audience being representative of the present day. Orlando had experienced four hundred years of existence, acquainting us with the reforms of the day in the literary, social and scientific fields. In the midst of all these changes the only aspect of life which remains unchanged and unaffected by all these revolutionary changes is the nature of man:

> It took her (Lucy) five seconds in actual time, in mind time ever so much longer, to separate Grace herself, with blue china on a tray, from the leather-covered grunting monster who was about, as the door opened, to demolish a whole tree in the green steaming undergrowth of the primeval forest.

(11)

Harvena Richter writes that memory is an emotional duration and, with its interpretation of psychic states, has a magnitude and unity, hitherto unnoticed.[39]

Virginia Woolf utilizes the technique of the awareness of clock-time. *Mrs. Dalloway* had the chiming of the Big Ben and the bell of St. Margaret. In *Between the Acts*, clock-time is designated with the chuffing of the generator and the ticking of the gramophone needle.

The location for the pageant is outside a little English village, the centre of action being Pointz Hall. The Olivers had lived there for three generations—Bartholomew Oliver, his widowed sister Lucy Swithin, son Giles and his wife Isa and their two children. Mrs. Manresa and William Dodge were two visitors to the Hall. Miss La Trobe plays the pivotal role of organizing the show. A group of spectators witness the pageant and these are the people whom the director interspersed in her play. The pageant is a series of scenes from the history of England with each particular scene symbolizing the changing patterns in every era. During the interlude, the movements and thought-processes of certain individuals are traced simultaneously, delineating their consciousness and personal conflicts. They finally disperse and when they go back home, they continue in their habitual lifestyle and their personalities remain unchanged. William Dodge is the only person who is transformed and comes back to normalcy, liberated from homosexuality by the purifying influence of the personality of Lucy Swithin.

Virginia Woolf hated warfare and held the male sex responsible for these strifes. She vociferously declaimed it in *Three Guineas*. She wrote in her diary in August, 1938: "And at any moment the guns may go off and explode us."[40]

Miss La Trobe, the author and director of the historical pageant, was an extension of the artistic personality of Virginia Woolf just like Hewet, Ralph Denham, Bernard and Lily Briscoe. On the final page of *To the Lighthouse* Lily Briscoe realizes her dream as she succeeds in capturing her imagination on canvas, unlike Miss La Trobe who, in spite of her best efforts, ends in a failure: "She hadn't made them see. It was a failure, another damned failure! As usual. Her vision escaped her!" (75) A.D. Moody writes that since Lily had cultivated an aesthetic sphere outside the realm of actual life, she was able to succeed in her vision. The lack of aesthetic perfection of Miss La Trobe's pageant is a result of the texture of life as it is actually known and experienced which is an immensely difficult and valuable achievement.[41] Though Mrs. Swithin was the least intellectual of the characters and she represented a simple religious faith similar to that of Lily Briscoe, her love is all-pervasive and it extends even to the little fishes in the pond. She expresses a greater degree of concern for the children than even their mother. She is like an angel on earth, spreading good cheer and joy all around her. In *Between the Acts*, she suddenly experienced a sense of personal identification with Miss La Trobe:

> She gazed at Miss La Trobe with a cloudless old-aged stare. Their eyes met in a common effort to bring a common meaning to birth. They failed; and Mrs. Swithin, laying hold desperately of a fraction of her meaning, said: "What a small part I've had to play! But you've made me feel I could have played . . . Cleopatra." (112)

Bartholomew was still imbued in the past, in his memories of India. Tenderness or adjustment were not characteristics of his personality. Little George was mortally afraid of him and his Afghan hound. His relationship with his sister was not on desired terms. He desired isolation and catering to psychological approach in his interaction with young or old did not appeal to him, like young George, or his aged sister. Yet, we perceive a streak of this very same psychology in his opinion when Lucy desires to thank Miss La Trobe at the conclusion of the Pageant.

Mrs. Swithin also has a very salutary influence upon many characters in the novel, for example in the case of William Dodge, the complex homosexual, who finds himself at peace in the presence of Mrs. Swithin:

> And he wished to kneel before her, to kiss her hand, and to say: "At school, they held me under a bucket of dirty water, Mrs. Swithin; when I looked up, the world was dirty, Mrs. Swithin; so I married, but my child's not my child, Mrs. Swithin. I'm a half-man, Mrs. Swithin, a flickering, mind-divided little snake in the grass, Mrs. Swithin; as Giles saw; but you've healed me. . . ." So he wished to say; but said nothing; and the breeze went lolloping along the corridors, blowing the blinds out. (57)

Mrs. Manresa, "the wild child of nature," resembles Jinny in *The Waves*. She was always out for fun and enjoyment, catering to her physical needs but juxtaposed with a fearless approach to life, unlike the rest of the audience who had turned away from their own reflections in the mirror. Mrs. Manresa was a refreshing woman. Mrs. Bartholomew felt restored in her company, with return of his youth and spice islands. But in the precincts of her heart she was a lonely woman, desiring a child, as Virginia herself had longed for.

To articulate our inner thoughts and feelings is an impossible task for many. But Virginia Woolf is able to express her inner being along with infinite moments of revelation. She deals with her characters sympathetically, and her gentle taunts and sarcasms of the earlier novels are missing in *Between the Acts*. She portrays her protagonists with great maturity and is able to delineate them from both the individual and social perspectives.

McLaurin points out that modern art has brought surface and deep sensibilities into open conflict, projecting the tension between the outer and inner worlds.[42] Virginia Woolf's personality desired that the unconscious working of the mind could be captured by the future writers. She voices her thought in her essay *The Leaning Tower:*

> The leaning-tower writer has had the courage, at any rate, to

> throw the little box of toys out of the window. He has had the courage to tell the truth, the unpleasant truth, about himself. . . . By analysing themselves honestly, with help from Dr. Freud, these writers have done a great deal to free us from nineteenth-century suppressions. The writers of the next generation may inherit from them a whole state of mind, a mind no longer crippled, evasive, divided. They may inherit the unconsciousness which is necessary if writers are to get beneath the surface and to write something that people remember when they are alone. For the great gift of unconsciousness the next generation will have to thank the creative and honest egotism of the leaning-tower group.[43]

This is the uncultivated sphere which Miss La Trobe had desired to make fertile, a place which would be fit for existence by her personal groove of confusion which longed to see the lights of day from the sordid, darkened existence of sex and alcohol. Nietzsche has delved into this quagmire of insufficiencies embedded in life—he said that the desired truth may be a rift from life if it is aimed at deception, delusion and self-deception. The Woolfian artist however understands the double dissimilation that Nietzsche perceived those who will the truth, a will that in unasking all, still conceals its own identity as a will to death.[44]

In all her novels, Virginia Woolf has focussed on death as an intricat, part of life wherein the dead are ignored and life proceeds on its course. Emotional death and a temporary paralysis of feeling is projected in Miss La Trobe's momentary fear of her audience's attention slipping because of the sudden inaudibility of the play. But suddenly a cow mooed loudly for her lost calf, followed by the loud mooing of the rest of the herd: "The whole world was filled with dumb yearning. It was the primeval voice sounding loud in the ear of the present moment." (103)

In this simple incident Virginia Woolf tries to delineate and portray the herd-mentality of the group-consciousness and how it is affected by the individual-consciousness. In the novel, Isa is a happily married woman with two children and a palatial home. Her complex personality and entangled desires are projected in an illusory vein, portraying a tragicomic individual on the lines of the Ibsenian and Chekhovian heroines. Her lifestyle was staid and prosaic. She wasn't pleased with her rotund reflection in the mirror, she never achieved what she desired but was ironically surrounded by ghosts of convention like being "Sir Richard's daughter; and niece of the two old ladies at Wimbledon who were so proud, being O'Neils, of their descent from the Kings of Ireland." (16)

Virginia Woolf's personal and private life is reflected in the novel. It wasn't specifically religion but solitude and silence in which she attempted to protect her vision of life. In many aspects, she faced a personal conflict in her life. Lucy Swithin also viewed the world in a similar manner. It is to be noted that Virginia Woolf has projected various traits of her personal lifestyle in most of her protagonists. The boat did leak at times and these were her problematic phases—her attacks of insanity when she had to strain herself excessively and which resulted in these attacks of neurasthenia. She loved solitude and socializing and juxtaposed these polaristic traits very well in her novels. But she possessed an extremely sensitive nature and her fine sensibility revolted at times. Like Septimus Warren Smith, she was denigrated to the care of psychiatrists, a tribe she wholeheartedly despised.

Rosamond Lehmann, in her recollections of Virginia Woolf, has referred to her sense of duality. This split in her personality is reflected in almost all her novels as the conflict between the individual and the group. Thus:

> Also there are moments, particularly in *The Waves*, when her sense of duality in human consciousness—the I forever watching the I—gives one an uneasy feeling of a neurotic split in personality. The split has penetrated deeper into her last novel *Between the Acts*.[45]

Between the Acts is a novel in which Virginia Woolf has been able to achieve in an artistic manner the juxtaposition between the isolated individual and the group. Their psychological needs, desire for companionship, emotional interaction and sexual attraction are all intermingled within the little group. Isa's attraction for Rupert Haines and William Dodge, the mutual attraction of Mrs. Manresa and Giles, the attraction of William Dodge for Giles—all these were sex-based. The relationship between Lucy Swithin and Miss La Trobe is on the spiritual level. William's attraction and his immense love and respect for Lucy was an act of redemption. Individual grains of consciousness are integrated to form a group. Individually, they all require and prefer solitude but their psychological and physical desires and necessities have to be fulfilled and hence the need for social interaction. Miss La Trobe failed to convey her message and so went for solace to a public house. There was a spiritual disintegration between the legal relationships and socially acceptable relationships like Isa and Giles Oliver, Mrs. Manresa and her husband, Lucy and Bartholomew where a mode of unacceptable relationships also exist but which do not satiate any emotional desires. Conventions and social security triumph and are finally fitted into each of their own grooves of habitation.

Present time focusses on all the protagonists and their individual trials. She created harmony only while the pageant was displayed—momentary unity, significant accruing of attention only for a limited period of time. The characters are all experienced, mature and confident of the ground they are treading on. They are all aware of their circumstances and limitations, proving it so effortlessly. Silence played a great role in conveying messages. Lesbians and homosexuals are absorbed and presented adroitly, minus qualms or hesitations. Strong emotions of love and hate abound, criss-crossing the atmosphere with multitudinous emotions. Virginia Woolf made us aware of the present dilapidated, decrepit structure of society and in a vain attempt at unity, changes the narrative tone from "I" to "we":

> "We" . . . the composed of many different things . . . we all life, all art, all waifs and strays—a rambling capricious but somehow unified whole—the present state of my mind?[46]

Woolf projected this viewpoint by her favourite technique of juxtaposition. Here she presented the elevated personalities in history, in conjunction with the present-day commoners.

The village idiot was projected by Albert who is a part of ourselves and an integral part of society which cannot be treated lightly in present time. The masculine temperament, wherein the refined sensibility has no place and even if it is projected, as George's moment and epiphany while grubbing in the grass, it will be destroyed by brutal intervention, as symbolized by Bartholomew and his Afghan hound. Yet unifiers like Lucy Swithin compensate for separatists like Bartholomew.

Between the Acts is a novel which treats human consciousness as an integral part of normal life. This book is an optimum experience of group psychology. At the time of writing this book, Virginia Woolf was fascinated by Freud's *Group Psychology and the Analysis of the Ego.*[47] People feel uneasy in a group and the tension is caused by each individual's awareness of the other's drawbacks, facts which are observed but remain unexpressed. Communication in such cases is negligible and it is described very sensitively in *Between the Acts:*

> They were silent. They stared at the view, as if something might happen in one of those fields to relieve them of the intolerable burden of sitting silent, doing nothing, in company. Their minds and bodies were too close, yet not close enough. We aren't free, each one of them felt separately to feel or think separately, not yet to fall asleep. We're too close; but not close enough. So they fidgeted. (51-52)

But they do vibe with each other, only when they move out in pairs, projecting a fragmentary pattern of relationships. The ensuing pageant binds all the characters together for a short while. With modernization, relationships between people are also taking a turn towards individuation. As a result, social institutions are disintegrating. Most social systems are based not on true affection and adjustment but on a bare foundation of a social necessity. Universality is an invisible mesh, unifying the disparate elements, just within the least requisite relationship. The tremendous recognition of the individual consciousness is due to the development of psychology and analytical studies of life and society. When Miss La Trobe was attempting to convey her vision of life to a group of individuals through the medium of colourful and glamorous costumes and music, she was actually projecting bits of truth and life. Finally the reflection of the mirror shows the audience in a very effective method of intermingling the past with the present time. Social interaction was relegated to a minimum because, as in their limited social sphere, norms and traditions have to be respected and expression is restricted. The essential loneliness of individuals is reflected, complete with their love-hate relationships. Miss La Trobe's failure to project her vision was because reality was too strong for public portrayal. Fortunately, a shower of rain saves the distracted audiences from further ordeal.

Miss La Trobe had envisioned reality. Her vision was fulfilled as was Lucy Briscoe's, Bernard's and Orlando's. Virginia Woolf's association with the impressionist artists is well-known. She embodies certain aesthetic principles of Roger Fry, Mallarme and Clive Bell in novelistic creations. As McLaurin states:

> Yet Fry was aware, as we have seen, of the danger of the artist being too aware of his own processes, and for Virginia Woolf, who also never accepted any simple idea of purity in literature, the problem was an intense and continuing one which she related to the illness in society as a whole. But this relationship between art and society is precisely the problem, of the way in which we represent "reality," a problem which is ever new for the artist and which Virginia Woolf tries to solve in aesthetic terms.[48]

An individual's state of mind is processed by the environment of experiences taking place in the depths of the consciousness. Aesthetic pleasure should be an important fact of each and every individual's personality. One can thus understand and take delight in the artistic culture that surrounds us. The harshness of reality was transformed by a few moments of fantasy by Virginia Woolf. Her constant and intense struggle of living and simultaneously protraying life and reality was strenuous but cathartic too; because by projecting her thoughts and experience she released her psyche from innumerable pressures. Aesthetically too, her creativity gave her a sense of completion and fulfillment.

Virginia Woolf was not an impassive artist resorting to the staid and accepted norms of creativity. She branched out boldly and the culmination of this effort was *The Waves*—a silent novel. Beethoven too had made a radical departure from the traditional world of music. At that time people thought him to be insane. Initially all changes are received negatively, the appreciation follows later. The cognition of the author's aesthetic ideas requires considerable thought for complete understanding. But the artist's duration can never be outside the artistic boundary because the topic will invariably deal with man who is an universal being. Beauty in the life of society is the most complicated and delicate matter. Here, "the crystal lattice" of a beautiful structure is formed not by atoms but by people and their lives. It is no accident that the most elevated realm of aesthetic cognition of the world, according to the laws of the beautiful, is art as a social phenomenon. It remakes the experience of life into beauty. No matter whether the artist is concerned with suffering, heroic deeds, ugliness of comic occurrences, his work is a source of aesthetic delight.

Soren A. Kierkegaard, the nineteenth-century Danish philosopher, gave a graphic characteristic of a poet: "a deeply unhappy individual whose heart is filled with suffering but whose lips are formed in such a way that when a groan escapes them it turns into beautiful music."[49]

The novel does conclude on a visionary note, with Miss La Trobe's vision of reality. There is also a scene of reunion but the all-embracing mood of love is missing. The interaction between Isa and Giles is a routine affair which does not transcend ethereal heights emotionally but was on a purely physical basis catering to their bodily hunger. This too is an exclusive "state of mind" which cannot be disregarded. According to G.E. Moore in his Principia

Ethica, this attitude also governs our existence: "By far the most valuable things which we know or can imagine are certain states of consciousness, which may be roughly described as the pleasures of a human intercourse and the enjoyment of beautiful objects."[50]

Virginia Woolf was personally suffused with extreme reactions while writing this novel. There appears to be an emptiness at the core of her existence and this is portrayed and expressed by almost all her protagonists. Lucy Swithin who can be considered as the protagonist is the unifying principle in the novel "but we have other lives, I think, I hope," she murmured, "we live in others, Mr . . . we live in things." (53)

This is the real essence of what Virginia Woolf desired in her peaceful, harmonious existence, "a unified whole" depicted recurrently in her novels by the globe symbolism which signifies "a moment of reality."

NOTES

1. *A Writer's Diary*, 4th January, 1929, p. 141.
2. Virginia Woolf, *The Waves* (London: The Hogarth Press, 1951), pp. 5-6.
3. Avrom Fleishmen, p. 153.
4. E.M. Forster, *Virginia Woolf*, quoted from *Virginia Woolf: A Collection of Critical Essays*, ed. Claire Spraigue (New York: Prentice-Hall, 1971), p. 17.
5. Virginia Woolf, *The Waves: The Two Holograph Drafts*, ed. J. Graham (London, 1967); Quoted from Eric Warner, p. 103.
6. David Daiches, *Virginia Woolf*, p. 111.
7. *A Writer's Diary*, December 30th, 1930, p. 163.
8. *Moments of Being*, p. 117.
9. *A Writer's Diary*, p. 169.
10. Harold Nicolson, Review, *Action*, 8th October, 1931, p. 8, Quoted from *Virginia Woolf: The Critical Heritage*, eds. Robin Majumdar and Allen McLaurin (London: Routledge, Kegan and Paul, 1975), p. 266.
11. N.C. Thakur, pp. 108-9.

12. Maria Di Battista, p. 151.
13. *A Writer's Diary*, 28th November, 1928, p. 139.
14. Henri Bergson, *Creative Evolution* (London: Macmillan, 1922), p. 7.
15. Albert Camus, *The Myth of Sisyphus*, in *Existentialism from Dostoevsky to Sartre* (New York: World Publishing, 1956), p. 313.
16. Allen McLaurin, p. 52.
17. *Loc.cit.*
18. *A Writer's Diary*, 28th March, 1929, p. 142.
19. Bernard Blackstone, pp. 165-66.
20. Winifred Holtby, p. 189.
21. Avrom Fleishman, p. 164.
22. Howard Spring, Review, *Evening Standard*, 18th March, 1937, p. 10.
23. Allen McLaurin, p. 163.
24. Virginia Woolf, *The Years* (London: The Hogarth Press, 1984), p. 280.
25. *A Writer's Diary*, October 16, 1935, p. 258.
26. *Ibid.*, November 18, 1935, p. 259.
27. *Ibid.*, September 18, 1934, p. 216.
28. *Ibid.*, July 19, 1937, p. 272.
29. Louise A. Desalvo, in *Virginia Woolf and Bloomsbury*, ed. Jane Marcus, p. 112.
30. Herbert Marder, *Feminism and Art*, p. 141.
31. Avrom Fleishman, p. 197.
32. *A Writer's Diary*, November 21, 1935, p. 249.
33. Hermione Lee, pp. 197-98.
34. George Sand, *Histoire de Ma Vie*, quoted in Hermione Lee, pp. 201-2.
35. Avrom Fleishman, p. 192.
36. Maria Di Battista, p. 194.
37. *A Writer's Diary*, p. 359.
38. Edwin Muir, Review, *Listener*, 24th July, 1941, p. 139.
39. Harvena Richter, p. 212.
40. *A Writer's Diary*, Sunday, August 28th, 1938, p. 301.
41. A.D. Moody, *Virginia Woolf*, quoted from E.M.J. Latham's *Critics on Virginia Woolf: Readings in Literary Criticism* (London: George Allen and Unwin, 1963), p. 115.
42. Allen McLaurin, p. 50.
43. Virginia Woolf, *Collected Essays*, II, pp. 177-78.

44. Friedrich Nietzsche, *The Gay Science*, Walter Kaufmann, p. 282.
45. *Recollections of Virginia Woolf by her Contemporaries*, ed. Joan Russell Noble (London: Peter Owen, 1972), p. 66.
46. *A Writer's Diary*, April 26, 1938.
47. Allen McLaurin in Eric Warner, p. 38.
48. *Ibid.*, p. 53.
49. Y. Borev, p. 56.
50. Beja Morris, *Ephiphany in the Modern Novel—Revelation as Art* (Seattle: University of Washington Press, 1971), p. 188.

The Final Appraisal

Virginia Woolf can certainly be considered the most brilliant woman novelist of the post-war period. Her major concern was to create a sense of reality in fiction but her conception and attitude to reality differ fundamentally from that of the older generation of novelists. For Virginia Woolf, the novelist's view of reality as distinct from realism is subjective. To communicate this sense of life, the novelist must discard the construction of an external world and devote himself to the creation of character through a complex contemporary consciousness—a unique vision of the world—a web of interrelated ideas, a network of images and suggestions. Her notion of the group-mind or group-consciousness is "the luminous halo or the semi-transparent envelope," thus the need for Virginia Woolf to record the atoms as they fall upon the mind. The stream-of-consciousness of one character enables us to comprehend the individual actions of other characters.

Though a great deal of emphasis has been placed on the way Virginia Woolf has used the stream-of-consiousness method in her novels, very few critics have pointed out that her method is based on a tension between the idea of isolation and the notion of the consciousness of a group. The main theme of Virginia Woolf's novels is the relation of personality, death and time to each other; the relation of the individual to the sum of experience in general. James Naremore in his *The World Without a Self* has stated, "her books are full of scenes where whole groups of people share thoughts and become like a single organism."[1] A more detailed discussion is found in Avrom Fleishman who says:

> Not only are the characters's imagination stocked with collective images drawn from a larger community of mind, but the narrative employs these images to further characterize them.[2]

Again, in most of Virginia Woolf's novels, importance is given to the group-mind and its affinity to the mythical and classical past. Even the individual consciousness is schizophrenic where there is a distinct interaction and conflict between the individual "I" and the instinct of the group.

The tracing of the idea of group-consciousness in Virginia Woolf's work presents a major divergence from the stream-of-consciousness theory of William James where he is of the opinion that there is a partition between the consciousness of different individuals when there is a breach and a barrier between different personal minds. For writers who have adopted the stream-of-consciousness method, this isolation presents itself as an intellectual and emotional problem.

Though the main stress is on the individual consciousness, the tendency in the novels of Virginia Woolf is to depict the group-feeling which stimulates the individual stream-of-consciousness. Virginia Woolf's close knowledge of Wilfred Trotter's book *Instincts of the Herd in Peace and War* and Jules Romain's *Mort de Quelqu'un* is responsible for her interest in group-pscyhology, the crowd theory and the nature of the group-consciousness. This interest in group-consciousness is very obvious in Virginia Woolf's writing career.

Virginia Woolf herself existed in two worlds—those of isolation and society where she experienced very often a sense of alienation. It was mainly with the members of the Bloomsbury group that she was comfortable because she felt that it was a life of shared-consciousness. They saved her from total isolation and insanity during the First World War. To voice these two selves was a technical problem, transcribing her consciousness into an appropriate language, inculcating external factors of time, her being and the conscious sphere of the mind into two worlds. Richter terms it as "the voice of subjectivity"[3] and Freedman calls it the "lyrical I"[4] and identifies it with Tolstoy's "indivisible I."

The experiences of the self enrich the individual being when the past and the present influence one another wherein reality is diffused in the characters and mysticism permeates into a world which is recreated according to the individual perception. Her wonderful sensitive vision absorbs nature with its infinite details and individuals are portrayed with their complexities and variant moods. Virginia Woolf is a great philosopher delving into the cosmos, the unknown and returning with pearls of wisdom. The metaphysical spheres of our universe hold an infinite charm for her; even mundane happenings are visualized through the eyes of a metaphysician and very often the simple act of a falling leaf is symbolic of truth and reality. Social intercourse was not very attractive to her as she considered a lonely individual less harmful and non-interfering. She feels that it is only in solitude that one's faculties are creative.

As Virginia Woolf was an impressionist, sensibility and intuition are major facets of her consciousness. For her, value is to be found only in "the moment." She finds a pattern, a rhythm in nature and solitude, and her writings are able to infuse poetry into the mechanized lives of modern man. She directs our vision to the sea, the birds and the multifarious hues of nature. There is a common imagery and symbolism in all her novels and her characters are methodically grouped together and made to think in a similar way. Characterization for her involves the psyche, the mind of the character, which is nothing but her own projected thoughts, ideas and impressions:

> Her work is a pure expression of an individual vision. And for this reason we feel we can always trust her. We know she will give us nothing but the naked vision, the pure intuition.[5]

Time is a very important factor in the novels of Virginia Woolf and she handles the consciousness of her protagonists in the medium of time, like Proust, Bergson, Joyce, Faulkner and Lawrence Durrell. Time can have an infinite impact on the psychology of her protagonists. Joyce's *Ulysses* and Virginia Woolf's *Mrs. Dalloway* were of eighteen-hours duration. Faulkner was involved with the immediate "now"; Proust with a fragment of "pure time" and Virginia Woolf with the "moment." She makes time come to a standstill in the Great Frost scene—a moment of consciousness which William James compared to "a snowflake crystal caught in the warm hand."[6]

Further, Virginia Woolf has utilized the globe symbolism as a leitmotif in all her novels. It depicts a moment of time, combining the past, present and future. Hafley writes that Virginia Woolf sees the self as "the moment at which Orlando's awareness becomes complete and one is actually a communication of innumerable other moments."[7]

Impressions and experiences are moulded and shaped into the individual perception. As in Proust, past impressions are imprinted on the mind and released from the memory as controlled by the immediate emotion. The moment is symbolized as a round object, knots, bubbles, globe, a ring, circle, projected according to the character's mood and emotion. This is similar to Aristotle's doctrine of self-determinism where man is controlled by the forces operating within him and not merely by external force.

In Virginia Woolf's first novel *The Voyage Out,* Rachel Vinrace is an innocent inexperienced individual with a non-reflective consciousness. When she plunged into social life, she looked for deeper meaning of existence in the lives of individuals she had encountered. She however had to attend parties which signified disunity, pointless conversation and futile relationship. Similarly this artistic leitmotif is projected in Rhoda, Miss Marchmont and Septimus—the protagonists of other Woolf novels. It has been observed that these characters thrive only in solitude and in contemplation of art. Finally it is through individual contact that they conceive pure joy and a meaningfulness in life through human relationships. The rising of bubbles in Rachel's tea-cup and North's champagne, conjoining and yet retaining their form, indicates their strong individuality and disinclination to get wholly involved with the outside world. But Terence, while retaining his individuality, believed in group-interaction imagining that the bubbles would finally unite to form one enormous world and this could be achieved only in death.

As the individual's consciousness is the outcome of one's impressions which break or mould an individual's personality, our lifestyle monitors the activity of the consciousness. Our mode of existence controls our moods, memories and perceptions.

> To bring into one's own sphere of comprehension, into one's self, the enormous vision which the world and the process of life have to offer, to integrate the external, universal flux of life, death and time into the personal vision, is the challenge presented by the needs of Woolf's characters. Finally, it is in *The Waves,* with six characters sharing the consciousness in a world that is described by the author in terms of various stages of consciousness, the challenge is finally met. Death and time become part of consciousness, and the external world is reciprocally endowed with consciousness—yet there is not the stasis of a mystic consummation, nor does the individual self ever relinquish its identity.[8]

In *Night and Day*, Ralph Denham and Katharine Hilbery long for solitude so that they can pursue their individual interests, literature and mathematics. Schaefer considers Katharine's dreams to be identical with individualized and heightened human consciousness, which are vital for her liberation from the constraint of the social world, upon her feelings and her own natural tendencies.[9] Katharine has a rational bent of mind and Ralph possesses a mythopoetic sensibility. Mrs. Hilbery is the wise fool, immersed in the works of Shakespeare, yet beneath the surface caricature, she is remarkably perceptive. Mary Datchet is realistic, perceptive and self-contained. She identifies her personal identity with the feminist movement. Virginia Woolf's feminism influenced her considerably especially while projecting her views on society and the individual. For Virginia Woolf the self's creation and exploration of its individual world is a fundamental need, for her moral criticism focuses on that which hinders individual perception. Similarly her social criticism is based upon the way social responsibilities and modes of communication intrude upon thought and vision. According to Virginia Woolf, society itself has a limiting view on the thoughts of the individual. This attitude is very well brought out in Septimus Warren Smith's suicide and Mrs. Dalloway's conviction that he was right in his aggressive assertion about the social norms. Likewise, Jacob is a complex person, with a diffused and elusive personality. Woolf projects the insubstantiality of an individual, transient and governed by either life or death: "there is no use trying to sum people up. One must follow hints not exactly what is said, not yet entirely what is done." (29)

Jacob's extreme individuality can be evinced from the lines where he says that there can be no form unless he makes one for himself. Thus his affinity was with the timeless relics of Greek architecture, the Parthenon and the Acropolis. Individuality may exist in varied forms, wedge-shaped, nebulous darkness, inscrutable and unfathomable: "Miracles, revelations, agonies, loneliness, falling through the sea, down, down, into the flames." (157)

One's inner being's spatial existence is within one's body, capable of independent survival, negating the social world. But that inner spirit should in its entirety be sufficient to pervade him with a feeling of satiation and reality, or else: "one could keep step with the crowd and never be found out for the hollow machine lacking the essential thing that one was conscious of being." (272)

Clarissa Dalloway fulfils with flair her role as a social hostess, catering to her husband's official duties but she still leads a cocoon-like existence, with her emotions clamped in her heart. Septimus suffers from emotional paralysis due to shell-shock. The repression of his actual feelings erupted volcanically, disrupting and disintegrating all barriers of social norms. He rebelled against society, war and authority, and the compulsory humiliation and harassment by psychiatrists. Clarissa's inexpressed emotions were satiated with his single act of defiance. Virginia Woolf has succeeded in portraying the two characteristics of one person delineated by two individuals. Clarissa is the rational conscious being and Septimus the irrational unconscious being. "Sanity and insanity, Mrs. Dalloway seeing the truth. Septimus Smith seeing the insane truth. Wherein she tries to explain the feeling of 'falling through into discoveries,' while perceiving reality."[10] Peter Walsh experiences a moment of epiphany on perceiving Clarissa. He transcends his loneliness as she does hers. Her communication with Peter was on a better plane. People conglomerate around her during her parties, but her loneliness persisted, "But to go deeper, beneath what people said . . . in her own mind now, what did it mean to her, this thing she called life?" (444)

Septimus was an emotionally disturbed war veteran and he felt that he was "connected by millions of fibres with his own body, there on the seat." (32) He responded to nature favourably and identified himself with its serene simplicity: "The earth thrilled beneath him. Red flowers grew through his flesh their stiff leaves rustled by his head." (103)

Mrs. Ramsay of *To the Lighthouse* is an unique individual. She is unaware of her ethereal beauty, wholly engrossed in her family affairs. The dinner party she gave threatened to be dull, till she intervened and with her perfect touch she created an atmosphere of amity—the merging of disparate elements and creating harmony. She is a unifier like Mrs. Swithin, Mrs. Hilbery, Eleanor and Mrs. Dalloway.

In all these characters it is observed that the psychological state of mind determines the mode of perception. Septimus and Rhoda's psyche are elevated to visionary angles. Their extreme sensitivity is the reason for their maladjustment in society which leads to their innate desire for solitude. Septimus visualizes Rezia as a flowering tree and hears the birds singing in Greek. This is Virginia Woolf's personal experience when she herself had suffered from a bout of neurasthenia. Individuality is like the sea, like moments which like the tide, ebb and flow, which finally submerges us if we are unable to retain our grip on life. The fact of isolation is intensified to an almost unbearable pitch by the diction, style and meaning-complements.

Clarissa's and Septimus's basic conflict is between chaos and order, forming a set of symbolic leitmotifs that are interwoven in an infinite variety to produce different textures of meanings. Mr. and Mrs. Ramsay are ill-matched because the latter possessed a serene disposition while the former was a boisterous disciplinarian. Mrs. Ramsay's life had to be sacrificed at the altar of peace. Only then did the other protagonists attain their individual visions and they were all united emotionally. They felt enlightened and were bathed in the all-pervasive love.

Virginia Woolf's sense of reality is emotional—it was centred in the 'moment' which is a knot of consciousness—visual impressions which congeal into moments of experience. The story itself is an outer shell, harbouring reality in the core of the narrative. Dr. Susanne Langar is of the opinion that "feeling is the generic process of all mental experience—sensation, emotion, imagination, recollection and reasoning. Unfelt vital rhythms are ensconced by Virginia Woolf in her writings."[11] Language therefore plays a vital role in translating the inner thoughts and investing them with clarity on the ambiguity of life, attempting to mould this amorphous mass to meaningful patterns. Almost all readers are impressed by the exquisite artistry expressed in the prose style of Virginia Woolf. She has been able to develop a style which is delicate, supple, shimmering and splendidly expressive. She is adept at rendering elusive shades of thoughts and feelings, and she is therefore able to achieve the imaginative recreation rather than the formal dissection of human experience.

Life's mysteries are simplified by delving into the inexplicable forces which surround our very existence. Individualism is an important aspect of existence which is the essence of man. The beauty of life lies in living every moment to the full—like Jinny, Susan and Mrs. Manresa who created values for themselves through action. To keep alive our inner psyche, we have to preserve our existence by subject-object correlative:

> Alone, I often fall down into nothingness. I must push my foot stealthily lest I should fall off the edge of the world into

nothingness. I have to bang my hand against some hard door to call myself back to the body. (31)

Very often a feeling of unreality envelopes the person, obliterating and obstructing free perception. Virginia Woolf speaks through her characters in her novels.

> The word seems to be spoken by her own voice, outside herself.[12]
> Then it becomes clear that I am not one and simple, but complex and many.[13]

These are the many layers of personality which have to be projected in a coherent whole, to retain sanity and escape disintegration. Our interaction with society at times cuts us away from our moral lives and we flounder in the social stream, "abruptly a chasm had been cut in his course, down which the tide of his being plunged in disorder."[14] Then momentarily, we lose the essence of our individuality. Yet, amidst these destabilizing factors, the soul has to retain a certain degree of stability, extract something alive amidst society and retrieve a sense of reality:

> My roots go down through veins of lead and silver, through damp and marshy places that exhale odours, to a knot made of oak roots bound together in the centre.[15]

Virginia Woolf directs our view to nature, sharpening our powers of perception, leading us into a wondrous and synaesthetic world of reality where feelings are received with genuine emotions and physical reality and they become synonymous with a personal desire to realize our true selves from the social quagmire of conventions and conflicts. For individuals desiring a life of solitude, company is a barrier to their progress and this is expressed by Virginia Woolf in her novels. "Her life was so hemmed in by the progress of other lives"[16] that she wished that no one in the whole world would think of her. However, "there was no way of escaping one's fellow-beings, she concluded."[17]

Existentialists are of the opinion that individuals suffer a death in excessive social contact and are preserved in solitude. Dorothy Richardson's *Pilgrimage* is an epic on an individual's life in an ordinary mode of existence. Miriam Henderson the protagonist was essentially feminine, with a masculine intellect, a requisite for surviving in the patriarchal society. Similarly, in her novel *The Waves* Virginia Woolf pursued her technique into a more intricate pattern, by diversifying a single self into six beings. She has dealt with the conscious and unconscious and invested it with androgynous characteristics by portraying three rational and three irrational intuitive beings. Percival is the psyche, the supreme force, the invisible thread uniting the various aspects of the multi-personal selves, "The multitude cluster round him, regarding him as if he were—what indeed he is—a God." (97)

The children's experiences recur at critical moments throughout their lives. Virginia Woolf presents their world to us, with her wonderful intuitive powers portraying vividly their early sense-impressions and tender emotions. As adults, there is a momentary detachment and apprehension of the discreteness of things; their individual temperaments taking leave of the sense-impressions and are again reconciled. This is an integral part of social life.

Jinny is involved wholly with life, but only with the superficial offerings of touch and taste, attracted to glamour—"a crimson tassel twisted with gold threads" and masculine company. Susan's desire for a family, farm and fields was satiated. Louis became a successful businessman but was haunted by a persistent sense of meaninglessness; a chaotic complex-ridden personality. Neville is disheartened with society and realized that is was not possible to develop a totally perfect personality.

Rhoda has condemned humanity. She is fragile, transparent and emotional. Her outer self is like a marble statue, pure and serene. Inwardly, she is like a turbulent sea, frightened to reflect even in solitude—her fears and complexes stare at her in the face. Out of Mozart's music, a geometric design of a square upon an oblong, she visualizes her inner reality. Abstract objects like Lily's purple patch and Andrew's scrubbed kitchen table, signify reality.

The Waves is based on the schematization of the consciousness of six characters. Initially, their innocent childhood facilitated pure uninhibited interaction. With the increase of self-awareness, differences are visible. Worldly objects remain static but their individualities tend to be on various levels, creating contrary impressions. Thus, the need to diffuse the individual-consciousness with general society, or to isolate the individual and create an abyss between ourselves and society.

Virginia Woolf's novels are built around the theme of interaction between individuality and society. Bernard's source of inspiration and his secret of existence were phrases and stories. Language is the nucleus of his world of consciousness, the unifying factor of all differences which is the very root of our existence. Because without communication, man would be relegated to the stone age. Conversation is of primordial importance in society. Bernard's stories are like balm to spiritual wounds, diffusing truth and reality in the world of selfishness and corruption. He integrates all the characters in his consciousness and creates a multifaceted being in his world of consciousness. These worlds of consciousness, the invisible "I" and the unidentifiable selves "until she felt herself possessed of two bodies."[18] His consciousness is his life and he holds no illusions regarding his body which can be mutilated and annihilated by time. But death can never disintegrate his soul and therefore he welcomes death with courage. Rhoda embraced death to achieve some meaning outside existence, in the cosmogenic, ethereal lives of spirits.

Ostracism from society can be a living death, a lone figure amidst a swarming world. But when we analyze this stance from Virginia Woolf's angle of vision, this attitude is a buffer from societal pressures and dominances. For example, Mrs. Ramsay's yearning for solitude, or a part of herself escaping into a personalized world of thought, even amidst a social gathering. Death may be voluntary or involuntary but this is definitely a release from traumatic social situations. Insanity and death have been the focal point of many authors like Dostoevsky, Kafka, Thomas Mann and Faulkner.

Virginia Woolf did not present a horrific image of death. Even in Rachel's last moments, the eerie old woman in the shiny tunnel personified the fears she had about her social existence; but death engulfed her into peace and oblivion—which resulted in a symbolic reunion of spirits of Terence and Rachel:

> Psychologists are now attempting to integrate the dimension of death into educational and training programmes; future psychologists, psychiatrists and sociologists are to be given an opportunity to consider death as a relevance to their prospective life's work. Death should be interwoven to create an awareness in psychology.[19]

Death is projected from various angles and situations. Rachel Vinrace escapes from society because of social insecurity and extreme individuation. Jacob Flanders's death denotes Virginia Woolf's hatred for war. Septimus Smith commits suicide as a last resort protesting against societal norms and the resultant persecution of psychiatrists. Mrs. Ramsay's dedicated service proved all-consuming and all-sacrificing. Through Prue Ramsay, Virginia Woolf asserts that childbirth entails risks for every woman and she has a lease of second life which goes unnoticed by the patriarchy. Percival's end signifies that death consumes anyone, disregarding age or circumstance.

Woolf's personal sufferings, loss and disintegration of relationships, humiliation and agony caused by the innumerable deaths in her family, have caused irreparable damage to her entire psyche and a melancholic attitude was woven into her vision of life. The most traumatic moment which caused a massive setback was the loss of her mother at the crucial age of thirteen.

For Virginia Woolf, death was a permanent release from worldly pressures. Maybe these dark tunnels of nothingness gave her better cognitive abilities than the moving mass of people around her. Virginia Woolf, like most people, did not fear death. What we can gauge from the behavioural patterns of some of her protagonists was that they welcomed death, their extreme individuation motivated them towards solitude and their response to death was not of fear and anxiety but of relief. This indicates a streak of toughness in their personalities wherein they opt for the unknown realms of the universe.

Death pervades most of Virginia Woolf's narrations. Even dead protagonists like Percival, Mrs. Ramsay and Septimus Smith play their role in absentia. Nothingness is projected into enormous heights and the sensibilities of the other characters weave intricate patterns around them. Since they do not converse freely, the reader is the only individual aware of its immense importance. Man's life is governed by contingency and finitude and her craving for transcendence to the other world. Consciousness of death springs from humility and grace.

It is seen that the reality of death which persists in all the novels of Virginia Woolf is a mystical and compulsory happening. It appears that only in death can one appease the tumultous self. Of all the protagonists, Bernard was an incumbent Woolfian hero who came to terms with death. We witness the process of his maturation, his absolute access to truth and reality, relating his life to death.

It is observed that invariably the chief protagonists are affronted with death either physically or spiritually. It is by accepting death, the ultimate reality, that the characters attain an optimum degree of spiritual awareness, accepting life and death as complements of man's existence. The author relates them to her mental dilemma on an autobiographical basis. Her characters desire solitude and are uncomfortable in company because of their inability to communicate and adjust in society. But an excessive craving for solitary moments is also not natural. It is only in community that an individual can transmute his desire for action. To define life in this world, to understand the human spirit, man has to commune with people. But there are extremely sensitive beings like Rhoda and Septimus who were unable to adjust to the extreme rationality of worldly life. The alienation her characters experienced was immense. But this loneliness aids them to acquire a oneness with life,

"Outside the window were truth and freedom and the immensity only to be apprehended by the mind in loneliness, and never communicated to another."[20] Similarly in her novel *To the Lighthouse:*

> he looked as if he had become physically what was always at the back of both their minds—that loneliness which was for both of them the truth about things. (311)

Hermione Lee has noted Virginia Woolf's fascination for Freud's *Group Physiology and the Analysis of the Ego* while she was writing *Between the Acts.* This explains Miss La Trobe's relief when a herd of cattle joins in her pageant. The audience in the pageant signifies group-consciousness. Unity and dissolution are the antithesis of all her narratives. The mirror-bearers reflected "Ourselves." The audience was quite disconcerted at their own reflections; only Mrs. Manresa boldly faces the reflections. The characters are portrayed in compartments, forming a fragmentary whole with the "scraps, and fragments." Each individual plays a specific role in society and if observed keenly, a meaningful pattern like a mosaic can be traced. The cast and the audience in *Between the Acts* symbolize society and its inherent fragmentation. Albert the idiot in *Between the Acts* represents the Id which is a hidden facet in the unconscious. He is a very private person, differing from the rest of the community, having independent values, projecting an extreme sense of individualization. Society stigmatizes him with various labels of insanity and he is thus alienated from society. Autism and intesne solipsism disrupts normal behaviour. People of this type are unaware even of temporal and spatial unity but their subconscious thoughts are continuously active. Dostoevsky has also traversed the mental spheres of this category of individuals like Prince Myshkin in *The Idiots* and Raskolnikov's state of paranoia in *Crime and Punishment.* An individual's mental state governs his perception of the world. As Chambers says, the personality of an individual "consists not of homogeneous entity capable of gathering experience of itself, but rather of discrete moments of experience."[21]

In William Faulkner's *The Sound and the Fury*, Benjy the idiot has been projected by means of a chain of confused impressions and associations. The individual's inner state of being impresses itself upon his outer surroundings. Individual identity is not wholly governed by communal identity, but is inter-dependent. The ego is an integral part of an individual, catering to the demands of the Id and super-ego. This is the central factor, the fulcrum around which an individual adjusts in society. Society is a multi-structured group and therefore the individual has to develop himself and integrate his qualities, feelings and desires to a productive whole, to play his societal role successfully which is the psycho-social commitment of man.

According to Virginia Woolf marriage is portrayed as a tension-ridden institution, the woman attempting to adjust all the way. At times it has been magnified to a state of oppression. Rachel was of the opinion that in marriage, "we bring out the worst in each other—we should live separate."[22]

Katharine and Ralph finally agree to get married with the understanding that each will respect the other's privacy. An ideology of feminism is based on social regeneration which was adopted only by people with broad-based principles of life. Between Isa and Giles, compatibility is negligible, yet they cohabit due to traditional pressures.

Buddhist and Lao Tzu doctrines preach the philosophy of detachment and realism. They had no charm for civilization but embraced nature with the trusting innocence of children. In their metaphysical existence they rely on intuition and meditation for a peaceful living. Jacob too had similar personality-traits but the war claimed him. He attempted to discover truth and reality in solitude; protect his individuality and escape from social gatherings. Septimus literally communed with nature but his uncompromising individuality annihilated him.

Henry James in his novel *The Sacred Fount* portrayed May Servier, the chief protagonist, as wholly involved with her family but emotionally and physically drained. Mrs. Ramsay was also in a similar situation, and she ultimately finds release in death. In *The Years*, Virginia Woolf has touched the grave problem of damage done to the individual by society. Eleanor is an individual struggling against servitude. She has for the first time dealt with a deformed male with his inherent qualities of rationalism and egotism. The author may have been indirectly attempting to release herself from her social bonds. Eleanor fails to do so; Peggy and North frankly assert their disgust of traditional norms and old-fashioned sentiments. Life was a temporary affair, fragmentary and discrete, like the bubbles in North's glass of champagne. Maud Bodkin expresses a similar view: "verbalization of physical realities creates an organic response on the instinctual or unconscious level."[23]

Adler's most primary psychological system was developed in the social direction. This is the most important factor considered in his study of *Individual Psychology:* "An individual's feelings of inferiority, according to Adler, were relative to the social situation."[24]

In the social context, the difference between the theories of Adler and Freud, was a single viewpoint. Adler gave excessive importance to society considering it a singular reality which was the nucleus of existence. But Freud initially disregarded society as an integral factor of external reality. Only in his last formulation in 1938 did Freud finally define the external world, or reality, as including society. Speaking with reference to the neurotic ego, he said: "It is no longer able to fulfill the task set to it by the external world (including human society)."[25]

Transcending the limitations of one's self is the initial step towards developing social interest, creating a social feeling, and an empathy with people around you which will be the advent of sincere social communion. Society harbours certain immanent customs and traditions which are laudable and some which degenerate relationships. The extreme cases of degeneration are the cases of neurasthenia, individuals whose consciousness has failed to identify with the social consciousness of society. It has become imperative for an individual to relate himself to societal demands.

Solomon E. Asch, in his theories on Gestalt Psychology, explains his idea relating to social interest:

> One fundamental source of the need for society is the active and the insightful relation of men to their surroundings. Our intellectual and emotional capacities urge into the surroundings. . . . To recognize the nature of a situation is to be responsive to its requirements. . . . This trend comes to clearest expression in the social relation. Our grasp of the properties of a person . . . awakens the need to understand, act, and care. In this sense, the striving for society is "natural."

When we consider socializing from a wider perspective, complete participation does not entail constant physical interaction. Philosophers and artists contribute towards social regeneration through the medium of their thoughts and art. This can be achieved mostly through solitude enabling the individual to gather his ideas by temporary segregation. Virginia Woolf projected this viewpoint by portraying this concept directly in the characters of Bernard and Lucy Briscoe, a writer and a painter, and Miss La Trobe, a dramatist. Even otherwise, she portrayed them as individuals leading normal lives wherein women were restricted to the hearth and home like Rachel Vinrace, Rhoda and Mrs. Dalloway. There was a hint of internal poetics within these women which remained unexpressed.

One very essential aspect of social consciousness is for the individual to develop the ability to identify himself with other individuals which constitute society. Developing empathy towards social situations should be the primary urge of an individual which will attribute to social adjustment and will ensure harmonious existence amidst society. Man is basically a social being and his consciousness automatically reaches out to interact with people around him. This is an inherent attribute and therefore socializing is an inborn trait which is also requisite for normal survival on earth.

Virginia Woolf's characters identified themselves with even nature, especially prevalent in characters who preferred social individuation. They feel socially alienated because their psyche can strike no rapport with the many social demands and customs. To retain perfect mental health, one should maintain a harmonious relation between one's inner being and society because man is born to be a social animal.

To ensure emotional balance, social harmony must prevail and this will happen only when our inner forces which are judiciously counteracted accept social principles and norms; pressures are reduced thereby making way for social interaction. Simultaneously certain inferiority and superiority complexes will congeal into positive feelings, overcoming all emotional conflicts and the individual will emerge with a whole personality. The psychology of man cannot be perceived. It is an invisible phenomenon but these ultra-psychic powers contribute considerably to man's existence.

Virginia Woolf's philosophy of life, thoughts, feelings, her whole personality are embodied in her characters. The heart-beat, the pulse-throb of each protagonist was her very own; every thought projected, every tear shed was from the abyss of her heart. Her tragic encounter of the patriarchy in the field of education, personal rights and sex was unsettling, resulting in frequent bouts of depression With these destructive influences, she became somewhat of a paranoid. She was obsessed with the desire to project her visionary self, along with her social consciousness. Therefore, her novels are generally built around the theme of individuality and society. For Virginia Woolf, human isolation is the supreme mystery and tolerance is the supreme social virtue. Beethoven's and Ibsen's works were hymns to solitude. Marilyn Zorn confirms Virginia Woolf's interest in the individual and group-consciousness:

> the rarest and finest thing she knew—her affirmation of the artist's vision, his great gift to the individual and society: to hold up for one timeless moment the mirror of Reality and catch there the human soul, creating by the radiance of the vision—Harmony.[77]

For Virginia Woolf, it was from the very beginning that she

descended into the inner beings of her protagonists, their consciousness and individual complexities. There is a penetration beyond the social existence, delving into the bleakness of the individual soul. The Woolfian universe was pervaded by the consciousness of her protagonists. Mrs. Dalloway and Mrs. Ramsay were caught between two worlds of consciousness but successfully established meaningful relationships. Septimus Smith, Rhoda and Miss La Trobe are caught in the world of neurotic loneliness. The women in Angus Wilson's novels too are a prey to anxiety, psychological break-down and even lunacy. Meg Elliot of the *Middle Age of Mrs. Elliot* continues her social existence, even after her husband's death. Sylvia Calvert of *Late Call* too takes a decision like Mrs. Dalloway, to adjust between socializing and retaining her individuality and the privacy of the soul. To both Virginia Woolf and Angus Wilson, divinity was denoted by a moment of epiphany, a moment of truth—a revelation of an individual consciousness.

Linearity and rationality can hold no sway in the precious moments of divinity which Virginia Woolf has ensconced in the heart of her novels. These moments do not lend themselves to analysis and language; yet she has achieved infinite success in embodying them in lyricism and timelessness. It is most difficult and painful to establish the balance between remembrance and forgetfulness, memory and oblivion. Virginia Woolf's great theme like that of Marcel Proust is spiritual recuperation through a rescued image of the past recaptured. Nothing can explain Virginia Woolf's vision of transfigured reality and death better than T.S. Eliot's *Burnt Norton* which portrays this timeless suspension of life:

> Words move, music moves
> Only in time; but that which is only living
> Can only die. Words, after speech reach
> Into the silence. Only by the form, the pattern
> The stillness, as a Chinese jar still
> Moves perpetualy in its stillness.[28]

NOTES

1. James Naremore, p. 73.
2. Avrom Fleishman, p. 84.
3. Harvena Richter, p. 130.
4. Ralph Freedman, p. 33
5. Bernard Blackstone, p. 245.
6. William James, *Principles of Psychology* (New York: H. Holt, 1890), p. 160
7. James Hafley, *The Glass Roof: Virginia Woolf as Novelist* (Berkeley: University of California Press, 1954), p. 98.
8. T.E. Apter, p. 3.
9. Josephine O'Brien Schaefer, p. 57.
10. *Dalloway Note Book I* (October, 1922), quoted from Harvena Richter, p. 120.
11. S.K. Langer, *Philosophical Sketches* (London: Oxford University Press, 1962), p. 11.
12. *To The Lighthouse*, p. 17.
13. *The Waves*, p. 55.
14. *Night and Day*, p. 407.
15. *Ibid.*, p. 69.
16. *Ibid.*, p. 107.
17. *Loc. cit.*
18. *Ibid.*, p. 407.
19. Robert Kastenbaum, p. 273.
20. *Night and Day*, p. 502.
21. R.L. Chambers, p. 77.
22. *The Voyage Out*, p. 241.
23. Maud Bodkins, *Archetypal Patterns in Poetry* (London: Oxford University Press, 1963), p. 113.
24. L. Heinz and A. Rowena, p. 126.
25. Sigmund Freud, *An Outline of Psychoanalysis* (London: The Hogarth Press, 1949), p. 76.
26. Solomon Asch, *Social Psychology* (New York: Prentice Hall, 1952), p. 346.
27. Marilyn Zorn, "The Pageant in *Between the Acts*," *Modern Fiction Studies*, Vol.2, 1956, pp. 31-35. Quoted from E.M. Latham, *Critics on Virginia Woolf*, p. 119.
28. T.S. Eliot, *The Four Quartets* (London: Faber and Faber, 1947), p. 7.

Bibliography

PRIMARY SOURCES

The Voyage Out. London: The Hogarth Press, 1915.
Night and Day. London: The Hogarth Press, 1919.
Jacob's Room. London: The Hogarth Press, 1922.
Mrs. Dalloway. London: The Hogarth Press, 1925.
To the Lighthouse. London: The Hogarth Press, 1927.
Orlando. London: The Hogarth Press, 1928.
The Common Reader, 2 Vols. London: The Hogarth Press, 1929.
A Room of One's Own. London: The Hogarth Press, 1933.
The Waves. London: The Hogarth Press, 1931.
Flush: A Biography. London: The Hogarth Press, 1933.
The Years. London: The Hogarth Press, 1937.
Three Guineas. London: The Hogarth Press, 1938.
Roger Fry: A Biography. London: The Hogarth Press, 1940.
Between the Acts. London: The Hogarth Press, 1941.
A Haunted House and Other Short Stories. London: The Hogarth Press, 1944.
A Writer's Diary: Being Extracts from the Diary of Virginia Woolf. L. Woolf, ed. London: The Hogarth Press, 1953.
Virginia Woolf and Lytton Strachey: Letters. L. Woolf and James Strachey, ed. London: The Hogarth Press, 1956.
Contemporary Writers. London: The Hogarth Press, 1965.
Collected Essays, 4 Vols. L.Woolf, ed. London: Chatto and Windus, 1966, 1967.
Mrs.Dalloway's Party. Stella McNichol, ed. London: The Hogarth Press, 1973.
Letters, 2 Vols. Nigel Nicholson, ed. London: The Hogarth Press, 1975, 1976.
Freshwater, Lucio P. Ruotolo, ed. London: The Hogarth Press, 1976.
Diaries 1915-1919. Anne Oliver Bell, ed. London: The Hogarth Press, 1977.

Moments of Being. London: The Hogarth Press, 1978.

SECONDARY SOURCES

Books

Allen, Walter. *The English Novel: A Short Critical History*. London: the Phoenix House, 1954.

Apter, T.E. *Virginia Woolf: A Study of Her Novels*. London: The MacMillan Press, 1979.

Asch, Solomon. *Social Psychology*. New York: Prentice-Hall, 1952.

Barrett, William. *Existentialism as a Symptom of Man's Contemporary Crisis: Spiritual Problems in Contemporary Literature*, ed. Stanley Romaine Hopper. New York, 1952.

Battista, Maria Di. *Virginia Woolf s Major Novels: The Fables of Anon*. London: Yale University Press, 1980.

Beja, Morris. *Epiphany in the Modern Novel: Revelation as Art*. Seattle: University of Washington Press, 1971.

Bell, Quentin. *Virginia Woolf: A Biography*, 2 Vols. London: The Hogarth Press, 1972.

Bennett, Joan. *Virginia Woolf: Her Art as a Novelist*. Cambridge: Cambridge University Press, 1945.

Bergson, Henri. *Matter and Memory*. London: Allen Unwin, 1912.

———. *On Laughter in Comedy*. London: MacMillan, 1921.

———: *Creative Evolution*. London: MacMillan, 1922.

Berne, Eric. *Games People Play*. New York: Grove Press, 1964.

Blackstone, Bernard. *Virginia Woolf: A Commentary*. London: The Hogarth Press, 1949.

Bodkin, Maud. *Archetypal Patterns in Poetry*. London: Oxford University Press, 1963.

Borev, Yuri. *Aesthetics: The Sociology of Art*. Moscow: Progress Publishers, 1985.

Brewster, Dorothy. *Virginia Woolf*. London: Allen and Unwin, 1929.

Burgess, Anthony. *The Novel Now: A Student's Guide to Contemporary Fiction*. London: Faber and Faber, 1971.

Camus, Albert. *The Myth of Sisyphus* in *Existentialism from Dostoevsky to Sartre*, ed. Walter Kaufmann. New York: World Publishing, 1956.

Cassirer, Ernst. *The Philosophy of Symbolic Forms*. New Haven: Yale

University Press, 1953.

Chambers, R.L. *The Novels of Virginia Woolf.* Edinburgh, London: Oliver and Boyd, 1947.

Chung-Yuan. *Chang Creativity and Taoism: A Study of Chinese Philosophy, Art and Poetry.* New York: The Julian Press, 1962.

Crossland, Margaret. *Beyond the Lighthouse: English Women Novelists in the Twentieth Century.* New York: Taplinger, 1981.

Daiches, David. *Virginia Woolf.* Norfolk, Connecticut: New Direction Books, 1942.

———. *The Novel and the Modern World.* London: University of Chicago Press, 1960.

Donoghue, Denis. *The Ordinary Universe: Soundings in Modern Literature.* London: Faber, 1968.

Durrell, Lawrence. *Clea.* London: Faber and Faber, 1960.

Edel, Leon. *The Psychological Novel.* London: Rupert Hart-Davis, 1955.

Eliot, T.S. *The Four Quartets.* London: Faber and Faber, 1947.

Fleishman, Avrom. *Virginia Woolf: A Critical Reading.* Baltimore: John Hopkins University Press, 1975.

Freedman, Ralph. *The Lyrical Novel: Studies in Herman Hesse, Andre Gide and Virginia Woolf.* Princeton: Princeton University Press, 1963.

Freud, Sigmund. *New Introductory Lectures XXII.* New York: W.W. Norton, 1933.

———. *An Outline of Psychoanalysis.* London: The Hogarth Press, 1940.

Gergen, J.K. and Gordon Chad, ed. *Classic and Contemporary Perspectives.* New York: John Virley, 1986.

Guiguet, Jean. *Virginia Woolf and Her Works,* trans. Jean Stewart. London: The Hogarth Press, 1965.

Hafley, James. *The Glass Roof: Virginia Woolf as a Novelist.* Berkeley: University of California Press, 1954.

Hawthorne, Jeremy. *Virginia Woolf s Mrs. Dalloway: A Study in Alienation.* London: Chatto and Windus, 1975.

Hayman, Ronald, *Literature and Living: A Consideration of Katherine Mansfield and Virginia Woolf.* London: Covent Garden Press, 1972.

Heilbrun, Carolyn. *Towards a Recognition of Androgyny.* New York: A.A. Knopf, 1973.

Henry, William E. *The Analysis of Fantasy: Thematic Apperception-Technique in the Study of Personality.* New York: John Wiley, 1956.

Holtby, Winifred. *Virginia Woolf.* London: Wishart, 1932.

James, William. *Principles of Psychology.* New York: H. Holt, 1890.

Kastenbaum, Robert and Aisenberg, Ruth. *The Psychology of Death.* London: Gerald Duckworth, 1974.

Keen, Ernest. *Psychology and the New Consciousness.* California: Wordsworth Publishing Co., 1972.

Kennedy, Alan. *The Protean Self: Dramatic Action in Contemporary Fiction.* London: MacMillan, 1974.

Kumar, Shiv K. *Bergson and the Stream of Consciousness Novel.* New York: New York University Press, 1962.

L. Heinz and A. Rowena. *The Individual Psychology of Adler.* London: George Allen and Unwin, 1958.

Lenin, V.K. *Materialism and Empiro-Criticism.* Moscow: Progress Publishers, 1977.

Laing, R.D. *Divided Self.* London: Penguin Books, 1965.

Langer, S.K. *Philosophical Sketches.* London: Oxford University Press, 1962.

———. *Philosophy in a New Key: A Study in the Symbolism of Reason, Rite and Art.* New York: Charles Scribner, 1953.

Latham, E.M. Jacqueline. *Critics on Virginia Woolf: Readings in Literary Criticism.* London: George Allen and Unwin, 1970.

Lawrence, D.H. *Fantasia of the Unconscious and Psychoanalysis of the Unconscious.* London: William Heinemann, 1961.

———. *Why the Novel Matters.* London, 1936.

Leaska, Mitchell A. *Virginia Woolf's Lighthouse: A Critical Study in Method.* London: The Hogarth Press, 1970.

Leaska, Mitchell S. *From Beginning to End: The Novels of Virginia Woolf.* London: Weidenfield and Nicolson, 1977.

Lee, Hermione. *The Novels of Virginia Woolf.* London: Methuen, 1977.

Lever, Katherine. *The Novel and the Reader.* London: Methuen, 1961.

Love, Jean O. *Worlds in Consciousness: The Mythopoetic Thought in the Novels of Virginia Woolf.* Berkeley: University of California Press, 1970.

Marcus, Jane, ed. *Virginia Woolf and Bloomsbury.* Hongkong: MacMillan, 1987.

Marder, Herbert. *Feminism and Art: A Study of Virginia Woolf.* Chicago: University of Chicago Press, 1968.

Majumdar, Robin and McLaurin, Allen, eds. *Virginia Woolf: The Critical Heritage.* London: Routledge Kegan and Paul, 1975.

McLaurin, Allen. *Virginia Woolf: The Echoes Enslaved.* London:

Cambridge University Press, 1973.
Moody, A.D. *Virginia Woolf.* London: Oliver Boyd, 1963.
Naremore, James. *The World Without a Self: Virginia Woolf and the Novel.* London: Yale University Press, 1973.
Neumann, Erich. *The Great Mother: An Analysis of an Archetype,* trans. Ralph Manheim. Princeton: Princeton University Press, 1963.
Noble, Joan Russell. *Recollections of Virginia Woolf by Her Contemporaries.* London: Peter Owen, 1972.
Ornstein, Robert E. *The Nature of Human Consciousnes: A Book of Readings.* San Francisco: W.H. Freeman, 1968.
———. *The Psychology of Consciousness.* San Francisco: W.H. Freeman, 1972.
Panov, Victor G. *Emotions, Myths and Theories.* Moscow: Progress Publishers, 1985.
Poulet, Georges. *The Interior Distance,* trans. Elliot Coleman. Baltimore: John Hopkins University Press, 1959.
Proust, Marcel. *Remembrance of Things,* Part I, trans. C.K. Scott. London: Chatto and Windus, 1949.
Poole, Roger. *The Unknown Virginia Woolf.* London: Cambridge University Press, 1978.
Richardson, Dorothy. *Pilgrimage,* Volume IV. London: Dent, 1938.
Richter, Harvena. *Virginia Woolf: The Inward Voyage.* Princeton: Princeton University Press, 1970.
Sackville-West, Vita. *The Heir.* London: Heinemann, 1922.
———. *Knole and the Sackvilles.* London: Heinemann, 1922.
Sartre, Jean-Paul. *Being and Nothingness,* trans. Hazel E. Barnes. London: Methuen, 1957.
Schaefer, J.O'Brien. *The Three-Fold Nature of Reality in the Novels of Virginia Woolf.* The Hague; Mouton, 1965.
Showalter, Elaine. *A Literature of Their Own: British Women Novelists from Bronte to Lessing.* Princeton: Princeton University Press, 1977.
Sharma, V.L. *Virginia Woolf as a Literary Critic: A Revaluation.* India: Arnold Heinemann, 1977.
Spender, Stephen. *World Within World.* London: Hamish Hamilton, 1951.
Spraigue, Claire, ed. *Virginia Woolf: A Collection of Critical Essays.* U.S.A.: Prenctice-Hall, 1971.
Thakur, N.C. *The Symbolism of Virginia Woolf.* London: Oxford University Press, 1965.

Tindall, W.Y. *The Literary Symbol*. New York: Columbia University Press, 1955.

Warner, Eric. *Virginia Woolf: A Centenary Perspective*. London: MacMillan, 1984.

Woodring, Carl. *Virginia Woolf*. New York: Columbia University Press, 1966.

Woolf, Leonard. *Beginning Again: An Autobiography of the Years 1911-1918*. London: The Hogarth Press, 1968.

ARTICLES

Bowling, Edward. "What is the Stream of Consciousness Technique?" *Modern Language Association*, No. 4, June 1950.

Graham, John. "Time in the Novels of Virginia Woolf." *University of Toronto Weekly*, Vol. 18, 1949.

Humphrey, Robert, "The Stream of Consciousness Technique or Genre." *Philological Quarterly*, XXX, October 1951.

Maslow, A.H. "Frustration, Threat and Deprivation." *Psychological Review*, 48, 364, 1941.

Muir, Edwin. "*Between the Acts:* Review." *Listener*, 24 July, 1941.

McCarthy, Desmond. "*Orlando*." *Sunday Times*, 14 October, 1928.

Nicolson, Harold. "*The Waves*." *Action*, 8 October, 1931.

Roberts, John Hawley. "Vision and Design in Virginia Woolf." *PMLA*, 61, September 1946.

Rourke, C.M. "*The Voyage Out*." *The New Republic*, 5 May 1920.

Sackville-West, Vita. "Virginia Woolf and *Orlando*." *Listener*, Vol. 53, 27 January 1955.

Sanford, F.H. "Speech and Personality." *Psychological Bulletin*, December 1942.

Spring, Howard. "*The Years*, review." *Evening Standard*, 18 March, 1957.

Stimpson, Catherine, R. "Feminism and Feminist Criticism." *The Massachusettes Review*, Summer, 1983.

Swinnerton, Frank. "*Between the Acts*." *Observer*, 20 July 1941.

Weigert, ed. "Existentialism and Its Relation to Psychotherapy," *Psychiatry*, Vol. 12, No. 4, Nov. 1949.

Wilson, James S. "Time and Virginia Woolf." *Virginia Woolf Quarterly Review*, XVIII, 1942.

Zorn, Marilyn. "The Pageant in *Between the Acts*." *Modern Fiction Studies*, Vol. 2, 1956.

Index